## ADVANCE PRAISE FOR *I'LL GET RIGHT ON IT*

"An essential contribution to climate change literature, this book advances climate justice with voices not typically brought to the table. The urgency articulated in these itinerant voices is impossible to unhear and, I hope, impossible to ignore."
—**Madhur Anand,** Governor General's Literary Award-winning writer and director of the Global Ecological Change and Sustainability Laboratory, University of Guelph

"A moving, richly diverse collection that connects the dots between the climate crisis and our labour conditions. This collection doesn't shy away from reflecting the twin realities of dread and sorrow that come with working in a perpetual state of crisis. But it also moves us to process this collective climate grief through strengthening our bonds of solidarity. A powerful read for all of us trying to live, work, and resist during the polycrisis!"
—**Jill MacIntyre,** 350 Canada national organizer

"This collection sings through smoke, holding grief and humour with tender precision. We're welcomed as friends to witness the labour of living through climate crisis, where catharsis emerges from honest reflection, our DNA is found in trees, and hope dances peace into being."
—**Brigette DePape,** climate planner at Narratives and author of *Sun Compass*

"Poems in *I'll Get Right On It* arise from inside a wide slice of the workforce: a massage therapist, postie, teacher, sandblaster, even an invasive vegetation management technician. A call centre employee muses how people waiting endlessly on hold to have a problem solved are like how we're all waiting for "the fix" for climate change. A fisherman pens a new folk tune lamenting how a proposed mine's tailings will impact the salmon on which his livelihood depends. Presenting a more accurate picture of where we are as a society than either greenwashing corporate-speak or the environmental end-time doomsters, the voices of those whose jobs each day actually rebuild the world as it changes are well worth a listen."
—**Tom Wayman,** author of *If You're Not Free at Work, Where Are You Free? Literature and Social Change*

"I am moved and awed by the power of labour in all the ways this anthology honours and holds up. Navigating the bleak depths and the bright sweaty surfaces of daily life, this book gathers an incredible range of workers' voices, offering much needed lifelines and poetic corroboration that we need one another. Testifying to the dread and persistence, the weariness and the tenderness, of everyday people living with the grievous impacts of centuries of industrial-scale colonial extraction, these poems help readers to nourish the creative solidarity we need from the ground up."

—**Rita Wong**, author of *Current, Climate* and *undercurrent*

"As we continue to work through never-ending catastrophes, this book reminds us to pause, look at our colleagues and comrades, and see that we are not alone. It shows us the beauty and the pain of the everyday and leaves us with the feeling that when we are together, we are truly powerful."

—**Ana Guerra Marin**, Iron & Earth

i'll get
right
on it

POEMS ON WORKING LIFE
IN THE CLIMATE CRISIS

# i'll get right on it

edited by
THE LAND AND LABOUR
POETRY COLLECTIVE

foreword by ANJALI APPADURAI

Roseway Publishing
an imprint of Fernwood Publishing
Halifax & Winnipeg

Copyright © 2025 The Land and Labour Poetry Collective

All rights reserved. No part of this book may be reproduced or transmitted in any form by any means without permission in writing from the publisher, except by a reviewer, who may quote brief passages in a review. The publisher expressly prohibits the use of this work in connection with the development of any software program, including, without limitation, training a machine learning or generative artificial intelligence (AI) system.

Development Editor: Tanya Andrusieczko
Copyediting: Emilia Morgan
Cover Design: Ruth Ormiston
Text Design: Lauren Jeanneau
Printed and bound in the UK

Published by Fernwood Publishing
2970 Oxford Street, Halifax, Nova Scotia, B3L 2W4
Halifax and Winnipeg
www.fernwoodpublishing.ca

Fernwood Publishing Company Limited gratefully acknowledges the financial support of the Government of Canada through the Canada Book Fund and the Canada Council for the Arts. We acknowledge the Province of Manitoba for support through the Manitoba Publishers Marketing Assistance Program and the Book Publishing Tax Credit. We acknowledge the Nova Scotia Department of Communities, Culture and Heritage for support through the Publishers Assistance Fund. This project was funded by the Manitoba Arts Council.

Library and Archives Canada Cataloguing in Publication
Title: I'll get right on it : poems on working life in the climate crisis / edited by The Land and Labour Poetry Collective ; foreword by Anjali Appadurai.
Other titles: I will get right on it
Names: Land and Labour Poetry Collective, editor.
Identifiers: Canadiana 20250226448 | ISBN 9781773637440 (softcover)
Subjects: LCSH: Climatic changes—Poetry. | LCSH: Global warming—Poetry. | CSH: Working class writings, Canadian (English) | CSH: Canadian poetry (English)—21st century. | LCGFT: Poetry.
Classification: LCC PS8287.C58 I55 2025 | DDC C811/.608036—dc23

*In memory of Palestinian activist, academic, educator, and journalist Refaat Alareer, who dedicated his life to poetics and justice; and Mi'kmaq poet, songwriter, and residential school survivor Rita Joe, who taught us how important our talk could be.*

## CONTENTS

Foreword .................................................................................................. xi

Acknowledgements ................................................................................ xv

Introduction ........................................................................................ xviii

| | |
|---|---:|
| A Warmth Remains, and Salt *by Hari Alluri* | 1 |
| Reverie: Canada Postie Winter Picket Line *by Ron Romanowski* | 2 |
| Tools — A Litany *by Jane Byers* | 3 |
| What If I Told You *by Jennifer Wickham* | 4 |
| remind me one more time *by Moni Brar* | 6 |
| Un día en la vida de un trabajador / A Day in the Life of a Worker *by Ivan A. Salazar M.* | 8 |
| Beaver Creek Bushwork *by Claire Gordon* | 10 |
| Building: A Psalm *by Kurt Armstrong* | 12 |
| untitled *by Kanin Gosbee* | 14 |
| where do you see yourself in five years? *by Alison Holliday* | 15 |
| voice *by Zahra Tootonsab* | 16 |
| Good Fences *by Jenna Butler* | 18 |
| Bad Kin *by Justene Dion-Glowa* | 20 |
| The Work of Extras *by James Croal Jackson* | 21 |
| 911 — This Is an Emergency *by Renee Cronley* | 22 |
| A Tender Tale (Foxtail Barley) *by David C. Brydges* | 23 |
| biox *by Kate Siklosi* | 24 |
| The Horses Still Need Fed Today *by Trisia Eddy Woods* | 26 |
| Deep Tissue *by Amanda Donnelly* | 28 |
| blue collar memories *by Duncan Mercredi* | 29 |
| Rise, Get Organized *by Levy Abad* | 30 |
| The Song of the Invasive Vegetation Management Technician *by Ray Owen* | 31 |
| Rooing Fleece *by SJ Jones and Samantha F. Jones* | 32 |
| Waste Not *by Judy Parceaud* | 34 |
| Climate Action Is My Retirement Job *by Jean Clipsham* | 36 |
| Nechako (2000) *by Ella Soper* | 37 |
| Serving La Barriere Park *by Mike Bagamery* | 38 |
| Enduring Symbols of Disposability *by Kristian Enright* | 40 |
| A Different Kind of Summer *by Jennifer deGroot* | 42 |

| | |
|---|---|
| gas station *by Caitlin McCullam-Arnal* | 43 |
| Peasant Urbanite *by Sanita Fejzić* | 44 |
| No *by Dani Spinosa* | 46 |
| in vancouver *by Leah McInnis* | 47 |
| Due Diligence Is No Defence *by Lisa Mulrooney* | 48 |
| Mothballing Mould Bay, NWT *by Kelly Shepherd* | 50 |
| Fire Season *by Jessica Smithies* | 51 |
| Bitumen Refining and Its Outcomes: A Short Course *by Ross Belot* | 52 |
| Roofer *by Sabrina Spenser Smith* | 55 |
| 988 *by Fiona Conway* | 56 |
| Carbon Offsets *by Rina Garcia Chua* | 57 |
| Sweltering College Classrooms *by Catherine Parceaud* | 58 |
| Wiininaamowin, Air Pollution *by Renée E. Mazinegiizhigoo-kwe Bédard* | 60 |
| Into the Coulee *by Evan Woelk Balzer* | 62 |
| Barry *by Brad Fougere* | 63 |
| Bootstraps *by Jim Daniels* | 64 |
| Work Words Work *by Marjorie Poor* | 66 |
| Coffee Centre Call Shop *by Luana Terán* | 67 |
| Nice People Weather Speak *by Lena Palacios* | 68 |
| An Energy-Conscious Workplace *by Bonnie Quan Symons* | 70 |
| We Sleep with the Windows Closed *by Yolanda Hansen* | 71 |
| The Advocate *by Ikeoluwapo B. Baruwa* | 72 |
| Closing Shift — 2525 Main St. — 11/9/2020 *by Olivia Ingram* | 73 |
| Climate Adversity *by Lance Guilbault* | 74 |
| Be a Security Professional *by Martin Durkin* | 76 |
| I Strap the Suit On *by Rob Madden* | 78 |
| Professional Experience *by Jessica Bebenek* | 79 |
| Leaf-Murmur *by Christine Lowther* | 80 |
| Disabled by ME/CFS and Long COVID *by M.S. Marquart* | 81 |
| Islanders Prepare for Category 4 *by Credell Simeon* | 82 |
| The Aftermath *by Peace Akintade-Oluwagbeye* | 84 |
| Arctic Adoration *by Ashley Qilavaq-Savard* | 86 |
| Organizer's Car *by Alex Gallo-Brown* | 87 |
| Hold, Please *by Lia M. Markin* | 88 |
| An Inordinate Number of Insects (Field Notes from a Naturalist) *by Karen Loucks* | 90 |

| | |
|---|---|
| Last Christmas *by A.W. Glen* | 92 |
| A Distorted Portrait *by Paul Akpomuje* | 94 |
| Bad Actors *by Adhika Ezra* | 95 |
| inventory *by Christina Shah* | 96 |
| Hanging Lights at the Zoo *by Cole Osiowy* | 97 |
| May I Help You? *by Myla Chartrand* | 98 |
| Those Days before the Mine *by Jon Broderick* | 99 |
| Interview at Sea *by Lindsay Bird* | 100 |
| Turtles, where can I see? *by Mhao (em) Palevino* | 102 |
| A Prayer for Fish *by Hanako Teranishi* | 104 |
| entering landscape *by Ellen Chang-Richardson* | 106 |
| a farmer's lament *by Leslie Kaup* | 107 |
| There Has Been Something *by Ed Edmo* | 108 |
| Write the River *by Lorri Neilsen Glenn* | 109 |
| anthologist's haiku *by Melanie Dennis Unrau* | 110 |
| Undefeated: A Roofer's Haiku *by Gabriel "ArchAngel" Ehijie* | 111 |
| Good Indian *by Caleigh Miller* | 112 |
| Steamed Viviane *by Keith Inman* | 113 |
| Brooklyn-Queens Tornadoes *by Davidson Garrett* | 114 |
| appendix A *by Ruchini Abayakoon* | 116 |
| sacrifice *by Sydney Taylor* | 117 |
| the swarming hive *by Carla Harris* | 118 |
| Doing Reconciliation Work in Wînipêk *by Jamie Paris* | 120 |
| above epilimnion, warming too *by Tazi Rodrigues* | 122 |
| Emotional Labour *by Eesha Nilan* | 124 |

| | |
|---|---|
| The Contributors | 125 |
| The Land and Labour Poetry Collective | 135 |
| Credits | 136 |
| Endnotes | 137 |

# FOREWORD
*by Anjali Appadurai*

It was in the year or two after COVID-19 swept the world that I began to feel the prick of scarcity. It was the scarcity of mobility, as wealthy nations began to tighten their borders and my family and I could no longer bring over family members from India. It was the scarcity of refuge from the heatwaves, droughts, and other climate-change impacts from which I felt helpless to protect my family. Then, in 2023 the economy heaved, inflation spiked, and as a nonprofit worker I suddenly found myself experiencing financial scarcity too.

It's long been said that people turn to poetry in times of great existential uncertainty — loss, love, transition, death. Then there's the poetry that accompanies you while you clock into your job with a pit of dread in your core too deep to put into words.

We work to survive, and in working we are forced to uphold the economic system, with its contrived sense of scarcity, that rules our lives. Without scarcity, the vast, jangling machine of capitalism would grind to a halt overnight. Even if you're lucky enough to do values-driven work, like I am, there cannot be any illusion that you don't belong to the system, for you must uphold it if you want to eat.

In late-stage capitalism, we wear scarcity as a permeating stink, an omnipresent intrusive thought. In these pages you will find a line in "Un día en la vida de un trabajador" by Ivan A. Salazar M. in which the labourer heads to work at dawn "with the weight of dreams on his back / and bills that whisper like old friends." In "Reverie: Canada Postie Winter Picket Line" by Ron Romanowski, a striking postal worker yearns for the promise of a livelihood with the refrain, "what / if I had / a contract in my pocket?" Scarcity joins hands with precarity as employment becomes less permanent, more temporary, rarely assured.

And then there's the climate crisis, with its rising heat and its merciless inequity, covering us like a blanket with another layer of scarcity: the loss of home, the sirens of war, the precarity of wealth inequality. It's not just the wildfires and droughts — it's also the cycles of austerity and authoritarianism fuelled by the crisis. It's the ripened conditions for the renewal of fascism, for profiteers disguised as populists to take advantage of our fear. It's the never-ending march of land theft, shape-shifting colonialism, the ongoing suppression of Indigeneity around the world, the reinforcing of borders. Resource scarcity triggers a war and the fossil-fuel industry greedily uses the opportunity to raise the price of oil. We are told there is no alternative to the system that drives the crisis before our very eyes.

Through all of this, we work.

As the climate crisis makes everything hotter and more scarce, the stakes of work get steadily higher. In "Building: A Psalm" by Kurt Armstrong, we read of the overworked body with its "aching lumbar, sweat-stained pits, and stiff wrists," a reminder that the body is ultimately only tender, vulnerable flesh. We think: what a price to pay for sustenance. Christine Lowther's "Leaf-Murmur" drily captures how high this price really is with the line "Not like you have kidneys that will cook under heat domes." The crisis surrounds us while we are forced to work; in Lia M. Markin's "Hold, Please," a call-centre worker puts a customer on hold while "Wondering how much longer / I can ignore the heat / creeping through the cracks, / the quiet, insistent way / the world burns and burns / while we wait."

The climate crisis feeds off scarcity and the two build on each other, cornering and closing in on us.

But something else happens when we feel that way. In this constricted space we encounter life itself in sharp relief — the threads of day-to-day existence that implore us to live for the sake of living. We cling to the lifelines of our relationships with human and nonhuman beings, to the beauty of the natural world around us, and to the sensations found in the interface between our bodies and our environments.

Along with varied stories of work, the poems in this volume are filled with glittering moments of connection. In "What If I Told You," Wet'suwet'en land defender Jennifer Wickham writes, "our DNA is in the trees," evoking a brief moment of timelessness, the sense of a grand continuum. In "A Warmth Remains, and Salt," Hari Alluri lulls us into the rhythms of landscaping work: "Arrange, // arrange again, dig with hands and spade, scrape the roots, place, cover / over, pat." In "Nechako (2000)" by Ella Soper, amid the bustle of a forestry worker camp, "Gusts, sweetened by the mountain's top, / carry on their backs laughter, loud complaint." In "Brooklyn-Queens Tornadoes" by

Davidson Garrett, a taxi driver caught in a storm befriends his passenger: "my yellow canary becomes a tortoise // trailing thousands of honking motorists. / I introduce myself to my lone hostage."

This anthology is also filled with a steady resistance, a refusal to concede to the depravity of capitalism. In "Wiininaamowin, Air Pollution" by Renée E. Mazinegiizhigoo-kwe Bédard, the poet cries, "who takes care of the air? / i do! i do! i care! / i burn sage to decolonize it / to feed the spirit of the air." In "The Advocate" by Ikeoluwapo B. Baruwa, a health and safety inspector tells us why they so carefully examine our gathering places: "I do this because you deserve more / Because I know life doesn't hand out safety / Because the storms outside / The floodwaters, the rising heat / Are not just nature's chaos." Moments of care and of generosity offer us a glimpse into a world wholly opposite to the cruel logic of scarcity.

The poet, even in the heart of struggle or of banality, connects us back to life — for in these conditions of scarcity we are hungry for life. Poetry brings us back to the framework of our bodies, the only real place we can build anything from. If we let them, verses can be both a balm and a compass for trying times. As Audre Lorde offers in her 1985 essay "Poetry Is Not a Luxury," poetry illuminates our lives in ways that open new paths forward: "In the forefront of our move toward change, there is only poetry to hint at possibility made real."[1]

The hollow political theatre of today provides thin cover for the consolidation of wealth and power by corporate elites and authoritarian demagogues. It is an age of relentless extraction — from the earth, from our bodies, from our minds, from our creativity and intellect and spiritual depth. As those in power perform a garish dance of anti-intellectualism in an attempt to appeal to the everyday person, as oil-funded interests strike up a feverish chorus of "drill, baby, drill," and as the wildfire smoke rolls in hotter and thicker each year — more than ever, working people must reclaim poetry, because it is our birthright.

While we strive for material well-being for all, our spirits need nourishment along the way. Anticapitalist Japanese poet Kobayashi Takiji compared the experience of being a poet and intellectual while also tirelessly advocating for the working class to "holding dual citizenship."[2] In times like these, working people must collapse the space between these two worlds; today we all need to hold dual citizenship.

Luckily, we have help: the history of working-class poetry is rich and varied. It is a global movement, born in the first quarter of the twentieth century when capitalism was transforming the relationships between production, scarcity, and work, and formalized further in the wake of the Bolshevik Revolution of 1917. We can draw inspiration from the defiant anticolonial verses of Jared Angira, the melodic solidarity of Pablo Neruda as he writes of the plight of salt miners in Chile, or — especially poignant today — Langston Hughes' "Let America Be America Again," a powerful socialist foil to today's MAGA movement.

*I'll Get Right On It* builds on this legacy and deepens it to match our present circumstance in the heart of the climate crisis. This collection reminds us that proletarian poetry is for all working people, telling our own stories as we live through extraordinary times. In reading these works, we are bolstered by the courage and humour of our fellow workers, by their resilience, by their vulnerability, and by the knowledge that our fates are intertwined.

Here we may find reassurance of our united struggle. And perhaps, with the help of these verses, we may remember life, and through it, a renewed solidarity.

## ACKNOWLEDGEMENTS

We consider writing and editing poetry to be gifts and acts of friendship. In describing this anthology as a gift, we follow Mississauga Nishnaabeg writer, musician, and academic Leanne Betasamosake Simpson and her book retelling traditional Anishinaabeg stories titled *The Gift Is in the Making*.[3] If we give you a basket that is made in a traditional way, for example, the gift is not the object you are given but the ceremony of its making; the gift is the time taken to find the right tree, to offer tobacco for the tree's sacrifice of its life, and the process of turning that tree into something new. We are stewards of the gifts we are given, and by caring for them we care for the relationships that made them possible. We have many people to thank who were part of the making of this anthology.

First, we thank the poets who attended workshops, submitted poems, and agreed to publish with us. Thank you for sharing your perspectives, experiences, and insights, and for expressing your solidarity with other working people by being part of this project. Deep gratitude to the team at Fernwood Publishing, especially our editor and advocate Tanya Andrusieczko, for seeing the potential of this project and supporting us all the way through.

Thanks to brilliant author and lawyer Katłıà for being part of our initial planning and visioning for the anthology. We are grateful for your early advocacy to meaningfully include new poets and Indigenous and Northern writers.

Contributor David C. Brydges passed away while we were finishing this anthology. We honour David's passion and advocacy for poetry, and we are grateful to have known him as a fellow poet and friend.

The title of this anthology was inspired by a line from Hari Alluri's poem "Blessing Wednesday." Thank you, Hari! We are honoured by climate activist and politician Anjali Appadurai's stunning foreword — many thanks.

We are grateful to have been joined by guest workshop facilitators Ashley Qilavaq-Savard, Paul Akpomuje, and Adesoji Babalola. We also thank workshop host organizations Common Weal Community Arts in Regina (especially

Ibukun Fasunhan), In My Own Voice (iMOVe) Arts Association in Halifax (Sobaz Benjamin and Thomas Elliott), Western Manitoba Regional Library, Manitoba Energy Justice Coalition, and Queen's University.

Tom Wayman, Yvonne Blomer, and Kathryn Mockler met with us early on to talk about what it's like to edit an anthology. Thanks for your honest and generous advice in those initial meetings, and for answering our follow-up questions along the way. Special thanks to Tom for mentorship, advice, and connecting us to work poets across Turtle Island.

We thank Mark Nowak for his lecture on social poetics hosted by the University of Manitoba Institute for the Humanities (UMIH) research cluster on Ecology, Canadian Poetry and Labour, led by editorial collective member Jamie Paris. And we thank the UMIH for hosting this and several other events related to work poetry during the 2024–25 academic year. Thank you to Vanessa Warne and Ekene Maduka for all of your hard work helping us facilitate the research cluster.

Our call for poems and information about workshops was shared widely by writers' unions, unions, environmental groups, radical/progressive publications, and individuals. Thanks to everyone who helped get the word out!

We acknowledge and send solidarity to labour, climate, poetry, and arts groups whose work inspired us, including our own unions, the Worker Solidarity Network, the Canadian Union of Postal Workers, Indigenous Climate Action, the Migrant Rights Network, the Climate Emergency Unit, 350.org, the Canadian Centre for Policy Alternatives, the Council of Canadians, the Canadian Labour Congress, the FisherPoets, the Worker Writers School, CanLit Responds, and Labour for Palestine.

Deep gratitude to writers' unions and associations, especially the League of Canadian Poets, The Writers' Union of Canada, the Saskatchewan Writers' Guild, the Writers' Guild of Alberta, and the Manitoba Writers' Guild, not only for promoting our anthology and workshops but also for all the work you do to support and advocate for writers.

For funding, we thank the Manitoba Arts Council, the Research Office and Faculty of Arts at the University of Regina, the Social Sciences and Humanities Research Council of Canada, and the University of Manitoba Institute for the Humanities. Thanks to Mari-Louise Terblanche in the Department of Geography and Environmental Studies at the University of Regina for administrative support.

We would like to thank the lands and waters that sustained us during this process. Our work is made possible by the imperfect but still very important environmental protection laws that make the Canadian environment livable, and we were sustained by the farmers who helped to feed us during a complicated economic moment. We wrote, ran workshops, and edited on different Indigenous lands, and we acknowledge that we are treaty people who are working towards meaningful reconciliation that is based on social and economic justice.

Last but never least, we thank our families, chosen families, friends, and colleagues for their support.

# INTRODUCTION

> *Bless and bless*
> *the co-worker who reads my mind and throws me*
> *keys, the one who leaves a mess*
> *I have to clean, the one who snarks*
> *the second one to make the first one laugh. Bless*
> *I've been all three. Bless bucket and rake, bent*
> *machine and hole in tarp. Bless*
> *I'll get right on it.*
>
> —Hari Alluri

Dear Reader,

We are the Land and Labour Poetry Collective, a collaborative group of six poets, writers, and editors who first gathered in spring 2024 with a shared commitment to climate justice and an idea to make a poetry anthology about work in the climate crisis. The collective includes poets and nonfiction writers who work or have worked in farming, geology, project management, oil and gas, research, teaching, editing, and manual labour. We come from different provinces on the lands currently known as Canada; we belong to different racial, gendered, and sexual identities. Some of us are settlers, some are immigrants, some are the children of immigrants, and some are descended from Black Loyalists and the Black Refugees who came to Canada in search of freedom. The diversity of our collective has shaped our collaboration and this anthology.

This project is rooted in cross-movement calls for a just transition on lands now known as Canada. Decolonial, labour, and climate movements are calling for our transition away from fossil fuels and to net zero greenhouse gas emissions to be rooted in the principles of climate justice — Indigenous rights; workers' rights and good green jobs; migrant rights; global equity; righting historical injustices including land theft, slavery, and environmental racism; and generally committing to leave no one behind. Indigenous and decolonial initiatives for climate justice like Indigenous Climate Action, the Decolonial

Solidarity movement, and Sacred Earth Solar are resisting extractive industries and governments while asserting and building Indigenous sovereignty and renewable energy systems. The Canadian Union of Postal Workers (which went on strike and was mandated back to work in 2024, a year marked by government undermining of collective bargaining) is championing an innovative "Delivering Community Power" strategy that imagines post offices as hubs and postal workers as frontline workers in a new, just green economy. And the climate movement's calls for a Green New Deal are gaining focus and momentum, for example with 350 Canada's All of Us campaign calling for an Indigenous-led just transition funded by taxing polluters and billionaires. Despite these and other important initiatives, the cultural work of connecting the dots between movements, and between the issues of labour and climate change, is tentative and in its early stages. It is in this context that we imagined a poetry anthology that might help to do this vital work of connection.

## Why Poetry?

Poetry has long been a medium for resistance here and around the world, in part because of the way it skirts the market economy and circulates primarily as a gift. Poetry has played a role in virtually every social-justice movement, including feminism, the civil rights movement, the movement against South African apartheid, and opposition to wars, including the Vietnam War and the ongoing genocide of Palestinians. As a creative form in which the usual rules of language may not apply, poetry encourages innovation in language, expression, and ideas. It also serves as a barometer for the sometimes-unnamed but still palpable feelings or moods shaping our cultures and worlds. People turn to poetry to articulate shared feelings and build community in moments of sorrow, outrage, and hope; this makes it an excellent form for building solidarity.

Wherever there is work there are work poems, songs, and stories. As a settler-colonial country built on resource economies, Canada has a rich tradition of poetry about all kinds of work done both in service of and in resistance to the dominant extractive economy, including logging, mining, trapping, farming, fishing, rail work, domestic work, office work, hospitality work, factory work, service work, work in health care, sex work, and more. Alongside this tradition are equally long-standing traditions often excluded from work poetry that are based in traditional and cultural work, Indigenous work, racialized work, migrant work, and the work of anticolonialism and decolonization, antiracism, feminism, anti-oppression, and social justice. Poems about work circulate both inside and outside the literary establishment — published not only in books and anthologies but also in newspapers and pamphlets, shared not only at formal poetry readings but also at community and family gatherings, rallies, on personal social media pages, or in the midst of doing the work.

When we first met as a collective, we referenced Canadian poet Tom Wayman's work-poetry anthologies *A Government Job at Last*, *Going for Coffee*, and *Paperwork*[4] as inspiration. Wayman's foundational work as a writer, editor, teacher, and scholar of work poetry makes a distinction between poetry written about the working class by outsiders and the *insider* work poetry he champions — written by workers about their own perspectives and experiences. Wayman celebrates literary writing about work, arguing that our working lives deserve as much (if not more) attention than more widely accepted subjects for poetry such as love or nature. We spend so much time at work, and work determines so much about our lives, yet Wayman's point remains true: this aspect of our lives where we are often disempowered, infantilized, and exploited receives suspiciously little literary attention. This lack of attention serves the status quo of an extractive racial capitalist economy; this is why Wayman asks, in the title of his recent book, *If You're Not Free at Work, Where Are You Free?*[5] In our collaboration on *I'll Get Right On It*, we turned often to Wayman's anthologies and his critical writing to consider our commitments, methods, and selection criteria. We also had a sense of being part of a new, emerging tradition of work poetry.

It should not be surprising that the thirty-year dearth of work-poetry anthologies in Canada after Wayman's projects coincided with the ascendency and dominance of neoliberal governments, markets, and ideologies that have promoted individualism and market-based solutions while eroding unions, communities of care, and solidarity among working people. While corporations and governments successfully used an emphasis on personal responsibility (for example, in the form of individual carbon footprints) to distract from their responsibility for the climate crisis and their failure to address it, literary attention was also being diverted away from unfashionable thematic concerns including labour. A turn away from narrative poetry or the lyric *I* and toward postmodern and conceptual poetries in many ways widened the chasm between literary culture and everyday or working-class cultures, often marginalizing racialized, poor, and non-university-educated poets.

With the emergence of social media and self-publishing as new means for sharing poetry not controlled by literary gatekeepers, and with Canadian literature seeking a path forward out of its dumpster-fire era[6] when its complicity in racism, colonialism, and sexism came to an ugly head, we are seeing what strikes us as a friendly, collaborative moment in poetry. The poetry that excites us today is intersectional and anti-elitist, often exploring and reckoning with issues like environmentalism, settler-colonialism, Indigenous poetics, Blackness and anti-Blackness, and labour in ways that celebrate and validate lived experiences. This has included several ecopoetry anthologies — like the collaboratively edited *The Enpipe Line: 70,000+ Kilometres of Poetry Written in Resistance to the Enbridge Northern Gateway Pipelines Proposal*[7] and *Watch Your Head: Writers & Artists Respond to the Climate Crisis*[8] — and two new work-poetry anthologies, Amber Dawn and Justin Ducharme's *Hustling Verse: An Anthology of Sex Workers' Poetry*[9] and Shane Neilson, Sarah Fraser, and Arundhati Dhara's *The COVID Journals: Health Care Workers Write the Pandemic*.[10] With these anthologies as companions, we have been considering the politics and aesthetics of a work-and-climate poetry anthology adequate to our time.

## Our Process

> *How is the changing climate affecting your work? Has your workplace or schedule been altered by environmental change? Do events like extreme heat, floods, or storms influence your working conditions or pose risks to you or your livelihood? Have your wages or plans for the future changed? What are you doing to innovate or adapt to new or different work demands? Maybe you feel the direct effects of warming temperatures. Or other aspects of climate change might have more influence over your daily life — more frequent extreme weather, changing ocean chemistry, eroding coastlines, drought, shifting ecosystems, or pressure on health and wellness.*
>
> **—The Land and Labour Poetry Collective, first call for submissions**

We opened our initial call for poems, first issued in late spring of 2024, with these questions, inviting worker-poets to send us insider poems about how heat, drought, flood, fire, and other climate impacts are affecting their work. That first call also laid out our commitment to support and prioritize new writers and writers from marginalized and underrepresented groups. We encouraged submissions about the realms of unpaid labour, subsistence and traditional labour, care work, and social reproduction in which racialized, gendered, migrant, and other underrepresented forms of labour are often performed. And we promised poetry workshops to support new and emerging poets.

While we saw a good response to that initial call, we also noticed some gaps. Most submissions were from our writer communities and literary networks, with our efforts to reach working people through unions and other labour and climate groups seeming mostly to have fallen flat. And we heard from several people that they saw no connection between their jobs and climate change. Although the questions above were ones we knew we wanted the submissions and ultimately the anthology to answer, we realized posing them in this way assumed the dots we are seeking to connect with this anthology were already connected in common-sense ideas about work and climate change — and that's just not yet the case. We needed to step back and ask different questions to get the answers we were looking for.

By fall 2024, we had decided to extend our call, to make extra efforts to reach nonwriters and a greater diversity of working people, to welcome the submissions that were already coming in from outside Canada and reach out to work-poetry networks in the US, and to adjust our messaging to emphasize our belief that all workers are labouring in the context of the present climate emergency. Our fall posters, which we put up in our local grocery stores, libraries, union halls, universities, community centres, in labour and radical media, and on our website, read, "Hey Worker! We are seeking poems for an anthology about what it's like to do your job (paid or unpaid), make a living, or just get by in our age of climate change and uncertainty." This change in strategy created a boost, a shift, and more diversity in our submissions.

That fall, the editorial collective along with guest facilitators Ashley Qilavaq-Savard, Paul Akpomuje, and Adesoji Babalola offered a total of ten poetry workshops between us — six online and four in person (in Regina, SK; Brandon, MB; Winnipeg, MB; and Kingston, ON), attended by over 100 participants. We were inspired by American poet Mark Nowak's book *Social Poetics*,[11] especially his writing on the radical tradition of the poetry workshop, his experience facilitating workshops as part of the Worker Writers School in New York City, and his commitment to redefining working-class literature to include and prioritize writing by immigrants, migrants, precarious and underemployed workers, prisoners, refugees, and other underrepresented workers. We also drew inspiration from the poems by Worker Writers School poets that are included in Nowak's book — and used several of them as examples.

Although we designed and planned the workshops with a commitment to supporting new writers, it was through the experience of running the workshops that we developed a clearer sense of what that support might look like.

The participants encouraged us to consider how we would help them go from being workshop participants and new or first-time writers to becoming anthology contributors. We adapted our workshop design to include more examples of workers' form poetry (like haiku, pantoum, and concrete poems), which we found to be good entryways for new poets, and we offered to help participants revise their poems after the workshops. The people we met in the workshops shared their wisdom, their lived experience of work in the climate emergency, and their powerful poems, and we are honoured to include many of them as contributors to the anthology.

By the end of 2024, we had received far more poetry than we could fit in one anthology. We are pleased to share with you this selection from a large and growing area of poetic and popular attention and concern. *I'll Get Right On It: Poems on Working Life in the Climate Crisis* is a political art project that has caused us to rethink our likes, tastes, and ideas about what makes a good work poem and a good anthology. The poems in this collection are rooted in a variety of jobs and perspectives, and in a range of poetry traditions, from spoken-word to concrete, pantoum to free verse, protest song to storybook, and more.

## Connecting the Dots between Work and Climate

Not long ago, it was possible to speak of climate change as something that might someday impact the way people work. It is now clear that climate change is already impacting our daily lives and the way many of us work today. We see this reflected in the poetry of *I'll Get Right On It*.

Where, when, why, and how we work are changing as once-uncommon extremes become ordinary, weather becomes more erratic, and many folks gain first-hand experience preparing for or responding to more frequent disasters. Sometimes the connections between causes and effects are direct, as in the downpours and flooding a roofer contends with in Gabriel "ArchAngel" Ehijie's poem "Undefeated: A Roofer's Haiku" and the hotter-every-year conditions as a teacher and her students try to learn in Catherine Parceaud's "Sweltering College Classrooms."

In other cases the links between the changing climate and labour conditions are more nuanced, such as a young job-seeker making a white-knuckle drive through a "Storm of a century" for a job interview in Caleigh Miller's "Good Indian." Climate-related disabilities and health conditions can reduce people's ability to do paid and unpaid work; and global warming further endangers people with disabilities, as Sydney Taylor depicts in "sacrifice," which contemplates how climate events such as floods and fires pose unique threats when "hospital workers flee" and "my wheelchair won't work in the water."

Some industries are taking an opportunistic approach to climate change, extracting as many resources as they can while they still can, or expanding into new markets and resource frontiers opened by global warming. Ross Belot's "Bitumen Refining and Its Outcomes: A Short Course" reflects on this kind of work in an extractive industry ("We didn't care how they got it out of the ground. We were heroes"), followed by the disillusionment and grief that came after retirement and an awakening around climate change ("we were not heroes, I watched / California burn"). With the majority of mining companies globally headquartered in Canada, Adhika Ezra's "Bad Actors" describes the expansion of resource extraction in the Global South as "hungry men [swallowing] cities as vitamins for growth" and points to the hypocrisy of Canada treating migrants (including those from climate-affected regions) as "wastewater, the runoff / After *cheap foreign labour* has been wrung out of the body."

Seasonal changes and more frequent extreme weather events impact local tourism and modify farming practices and growing seasons. We see extreme weather impacts in Claire Gordon's poem "Beaver Creek Bushwork" about cleanup of the "seriously heinous carnage" after the bomb cyclone that hit BC while we were making this anthology. In Credell Simeon's "Islanders Prepare for Category 4," "Tourism stands in traumatic pause" — one of the impacts of Hurricane Beryl that Grenadian islanders have no choice but to "Bear." Trisia Eddy Woods's "The Horses Still Need Fed Today" concerns the unthinkable but necessary planning for "ways to evacuate a herd / of twenty-seven horses" in a wildfire, while Leslie Kaup's "a farmer's lament" hints at the adaptations farmers have no choice but to make in consecutive drought years.

Daily work schedules in industries like construction and agriculture are changing to avoid peak temperatures and extreme heat. At the same time, other workers continue to labour in increasingly unsafe conditions, while workplaces or labour regulations fail or refuse to adapt. Ray Owen's "The Song of the Invasive Vegetation Management Technician" describes a job the speaker says he will do for one last season and "no more": "By mid-July, the baking ground is belching H2S / And UV rays and wildfire smoke make Hell of all the rest // I'm swimming in my coveralls, their seams are crusted white / And it's been too hot to sleep this week 'til very late at night / But up I get at four a.m.; my debts won't pay themselves." Workers are drawing attention to unsafe conditions, and as temperatures, cost of living, and corporate profits rise, baker Levy Abad calls on workers to "Rise, Get Organized."

Some folks are working to mitigate the impacts of climate change through research, technology, revitalizing traditional practices, community work, education, and innovation in their fields. We see these kinds of work in aquatic biologist Tazi Rodrigues's "above epilimnion, warming too," journalist Lindsay Bird's "Interview at Sea," and Cree and Anishinaabe educator Lance Guilbault's "Climate Adversity," which depicts the absurdity of how climate change both affects his students' ability to learn and propels him to teach. Mike Bagamery writes in "Serving La Barriere Park" about his climate activism, citizen science, and acts of DIY invasive species removal. Others find themselves working in roles that respond to extreme weather, disasters, and the changing environment — from naturalist Karen Loucks's notes documenting the march of invasive species in "An Inordinate Number of Insects (Field Notes from a Naturalist)" to a front-line health-care worker "nursing refugees of / Climate crises / Corporate injustice / COVID-19 hellfire / Geopolitical racism / Medical disparities" while enduring the insufferably "nice" relations of whiteness in Lena Palacios's poem "Nice People Weather Speak."

Beyond labour that directly interfaces with the effects of climate change, many people simply need to work more hours or stay in unhealthy or exploitative situations to afford basic necessities that are increasingly expensive due to climate change in combination with other societal challenges. Kate Siklosi writes in "biox" about the tradeoffs of labour in the region known as Chemical Valley: "the orange glow of a good life: pensions and / scholarships and generous salaries paid / at the cost of cancers, death, settlement / payments and everything you could want / and need." In Myla Chartrand's "May I Help You?" a retail worker does a job to which she sees no alternative, thinking, "Miss when I didn't know how much trash there really is." The sandblaster in Rob Madden's "I Strap the Suit On" thinks about more than this specific job when he says, "this is what I do. / obliterate something to keep something else / from falling apart." Looking back on his work for Manitoba Highways and Manitoba Hydro, Duncan Mercredi's poem "blue collar memories" concludes simply with "my hands hurt."

When we consider the feelings and moods worker poets convey about work in the age of climate change, we note an undercurrent of deep grief and sadness, exemplified in Hanako Teranishi's poem "A Prayer for Fish" in which a server in a Japanese restaurant honours and mourns the life of a bluefin tuna, an endangered species turned into "pink gold" by the risk of its extinction; and Shosone-Bannock poet and storyteller Ed Edmo's observation "there has been something / that has disappeared / from my mother earth."

There is much to grieve, but perhaps the most pervasive mood of *I'll Get Right On It* is irony, rooted in the disempowering climate- and work-related feelings of repressed urgency, complacency, futility, despondency, isolation, shame, despair, betrayal, and dread. The current strategy of extractive industry, the billionaire class, and our federal and provincial governments is climate delay — setting net-zero targets without implementing the changes needed to meet them, while promising and depending on questionable and as-yet unproven technological fixes such as large-scale carbon capture and storage and geoengineering. In the poignant language of several call-centre workers featured in this anthology ("The phone is ringing" is an urgent refrain in Jessica Smithies' "Fire Season"), working people are effectively being told to "hold," to stay calm while the house burns around us. Meanwhile, Fiona Conway's poem "988" tries to respond to a child calling into a suicide line, "so afraid of the way / her breath warms the world."

Climate dread permeates every aspect of contemporary working life. As our bosses and our governments assure us that they are working on it, and that we are going to be ok, and as we are hired to convey the same empty reassurances to other working people, young workers like the speaker of Alison Holliday's poem "where do you see yourself in five years?" count their days and mark their calendars by ominous climate records like *"the hottest day of my life so far."* Smoke, wildfires, floods, storms, evacuations, pollution, environmental racism, and other threats form the backdrop of countless poems in this collection. It is hard to make connections, to build coalitions, and to do the work of fixing things when we are frozen with dread, yet it is under such conditions that we urgently need to do exactly these things. Throughout *I'll Get Right On It* we see examples of workers' ironic, ambivalent, frustrated, and bold refusals of apathy and despair, for example Zahra Tootonsab's use of flames and smoke to link students' Palestine solidarity with the climate justice movement: "we wreak / wildfires tired of your bullshit" and "I am the smoke of revolutions to continue / choking you out."

We find hope in poems that resist the ideas that no one cares or that we are powerless. Early childhood educator Mhao (em) Palevino sees promise in the compassionate children she cares for, the speaker in Brad Fougere's poem "Barry" contemplates organizing a union at the grocery store, and Jean Clipsham continues her raging-granny activism in "Climate Action Is My

Retirement Job." Artist Kanin Gosbee honours persistence and the shifts it produces: "Still, we persist // Another load of laundry / Cycles repeat, But change." Many poets find hope in the land — foxtail barley for oil sands construction worker David C. Brydges, a summer of gentle rain and blooming flowers after years of flooding and drought for farmer Jennifer deGroot, and gardening and writing as ways "to plant the seeds of peasant futurisms" for Sanita Fejzić. Inuk poet Ashley Qilavaq-Savard finds "clarity and vitality" and "the self-realization of resilience" in a "fierce" snowstorm. Such moments of kinship and care matter as antidotes to despair and points of connection among working people.

## How Poetry Builds Solidarity among Working People

*People forget that pearls are made from grief — jewelled evidence of wounds sustained while siphoning toxins from the turbid torrent of capitalism.*

—Eesha Nilan

The poems in *I'll Get Right On It* are rooted in the contributors' distinct and seemingly isolated insider experiences of the work it takes to thrive, survive, or just get by in the age of climate change. Like the pearls "made from grief" described in Eesha Nilan's poem "Emotional Labour," however, these poems are materially and analytically linked as individual emotional and creative products of the shared experience of enduring the conditions of life under late capitalism and in the climate emergency. Taken together, they demonstrate what it means to say, as Nilan does, that resilience "is cultivated among us not within us." Together, the poems do the important emotional labour of moving from the individual to the collective — a movement of social poetics that encourages working people to recognize common experiences, feelings, and causes. Like the image of individual bodies gestating pearls or poems amid the ravages of climate change, or like the string of t-sounds in *toxins, turbid, torrent,* and *capitalism* that resonates across Nilan's words and resembles a string of pearls, something resonates from one poem to another. It is in this sense that we see this anthology using poetry as a site for connection, for being seen, understood, and heard, and for forming shared analyses of power and theories of change — in other words, as a tool for building solidarity and climate justice.

Nilan depicts solidarity as emotional labour — a kind of work that is essential to the survival of our communities and ecosystems yet that is often racialized, gendered, unpaid, and underappreciated. While doing the emotional labour of making this anthology, we have thought of our work, similarly, as a form of friendship. We believe that in a climate emergency there is an urgency to the politics of friendship, rooted in a real sense of kinship among working people, with communities outside our own, and with planetary life. Friendship is more than a feeling; it is a set of activities, a way of behaving towards another, that is based on a desire for mutual flourishing. We must care about the suffering of people we do not know, who we may never encounter, and who are not even born yet. In short, we have come to a moment in time when we must treat strangers as friends.

The title of this anthology was inspired by a line from the poem "Blessing Wednesday" by our friend and contributor Hari Alluri. The poem is a list of blessings, or of things to bless — things that might usually be framed as difficulties or complaints about the poet's job or his coworkers. When Alluri writes "Bless / I'll get right on it"[12] he is both complaining about and honouring the ways workers respond to commands, to urgency, or to responsibilities fairly or unfairly placed on them. People who struggle to make ends meet, who are facing mounting precarity and insecurity, and who must work for a living have little choice or control over a destructive economy that churns out pollution and greenhouse gas emissions, threatening our communities and planetary life. Yet here we find ourselves, with our leaders, the corporations we work for and depend on, and the tech-bros who buy and sell our data bent on their profit and our destruction. "I'll get right on it" can be interpreted as an individual worker's expression of indifference, futility, resignation, or resistance. In the spirit of friendship and solidarity — and in the potential movement from *I* to *we* — it is also an expression of readiness. It shows that working people together have the power and the potential to organize, to care for one another, to struggle, and to "get right on" the project of demanding and building a greener and more just world.

And so, dear reader, we welcome you not just as a reader but also as a friend. Our hope is that, by reading this anthology, you will feel a connection with the working people whose poems are gathered here, and that together we will build our regard for each other and our wider communities, along with networks of solidarity, action, and care.

In solidarity,
The Land and Labour Poetry Collective

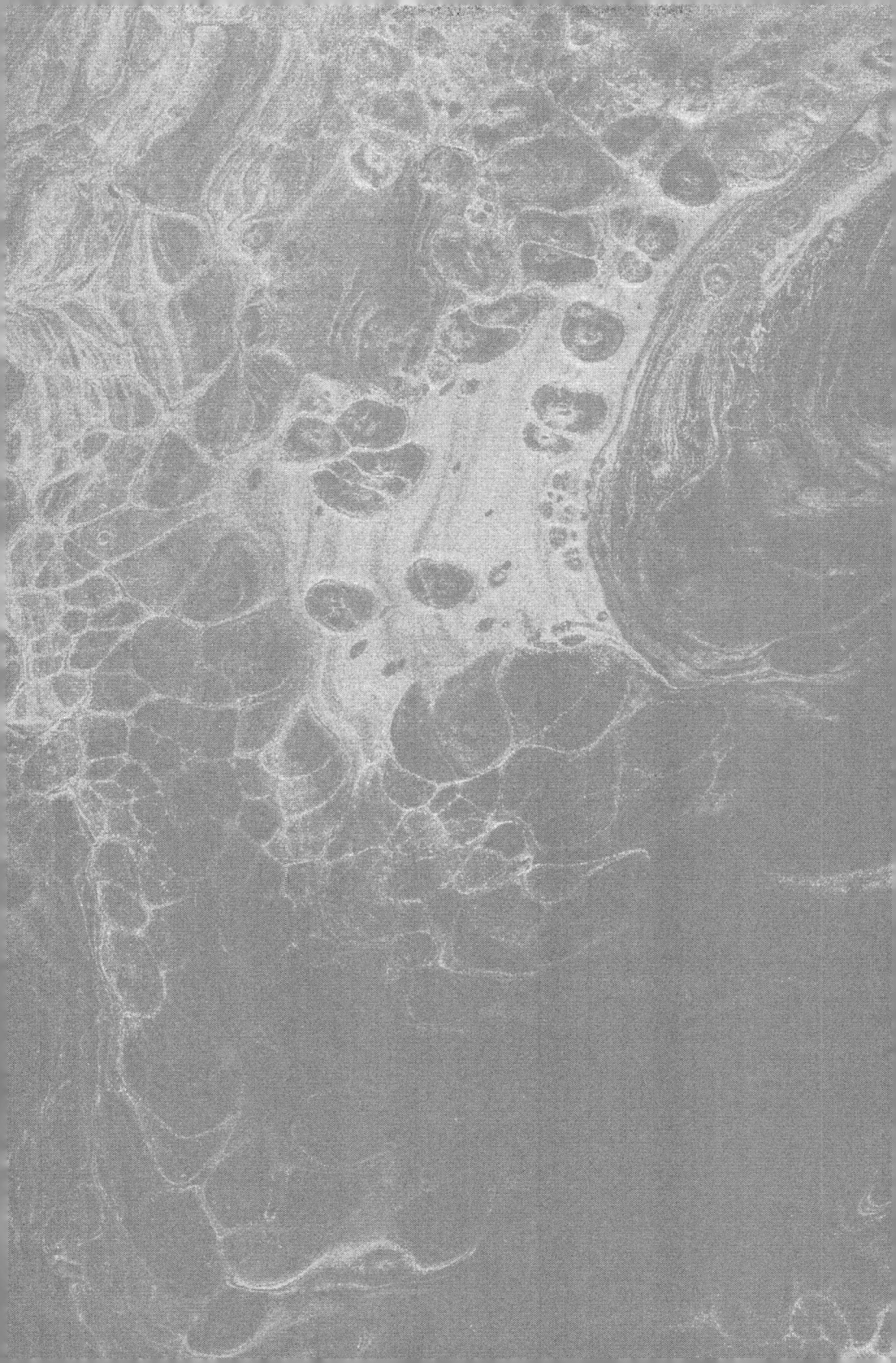

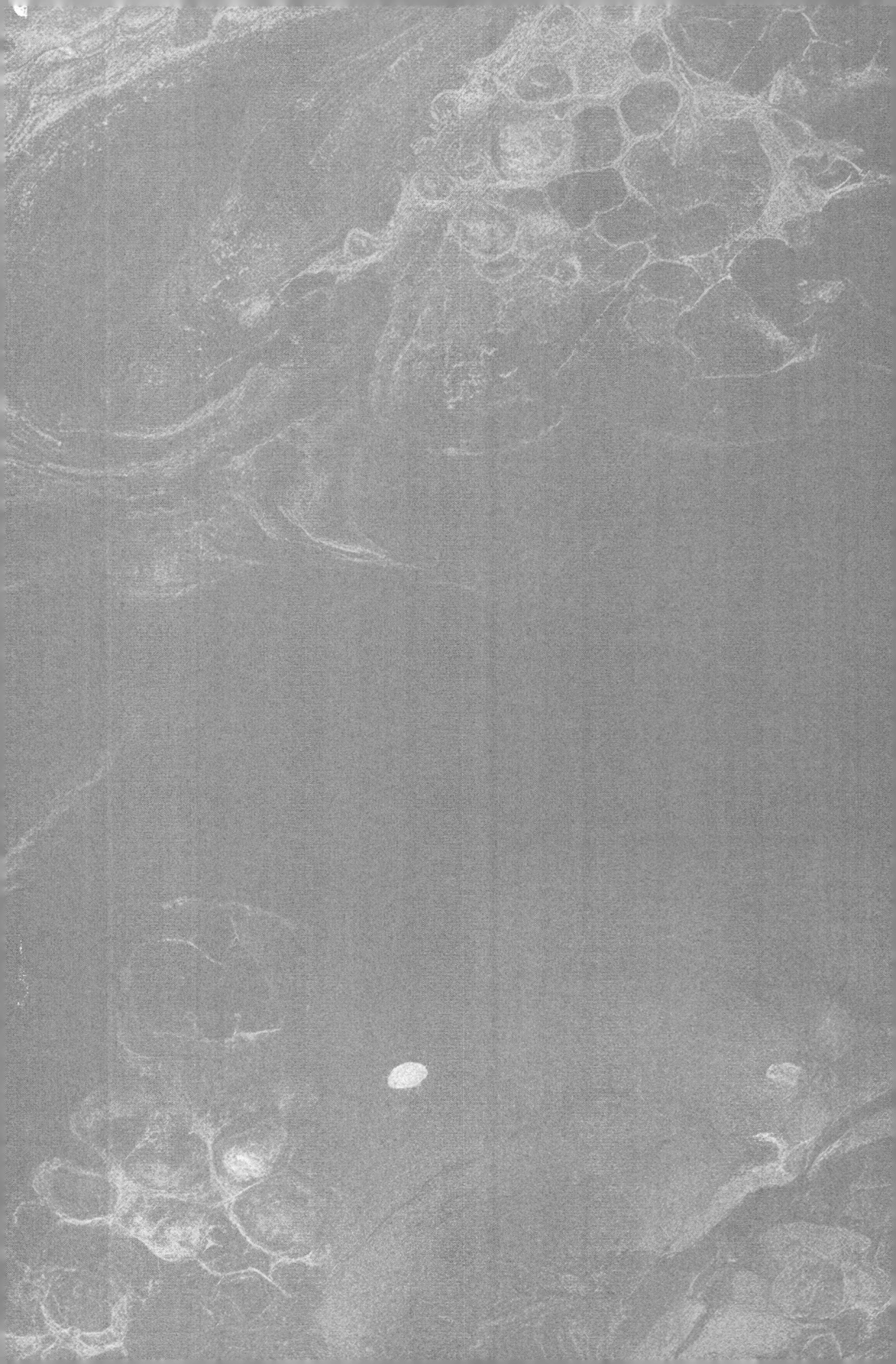

## A WARMTH REMAINS, AND SALT
by Hari Alluri

—*for Yannis Ritsos*

Our morning began as a hummingbird's window-stricken back-forth-
squeak — no WD40 in our truck to ease the handle's
grind and wind. Now, the traffic slows our highway swerve down to a nuzzle.

There's time, because for once the steering wheel is free of me, to read. Aloud:
my co-worker obliges with his one good ear, following the side-view
mirrors' guidance, holding to the lines Lolo Yannis weaves into my voice

en route to the city dump green waste transfer station. We are spoilt:
this Isuzu truck can rear up and throw off its burden without our tarp-drag-
unwrap-lift-repeat. "The heft of a mudra in my body," my co-worker

exclaims at *Diaries of Exile*, May 24. Our truck's tipper slides back
into its seat. Me, back into reading mode. There's no such thing as topsoil.
Three yards compost mulch, six wheel loader buckets from the waiting

pile to our truck. Through our shoulders' shovelling. Uphill via wheelbarrow,
elbows locked, and core. Leg it to a bed we'll rake and plant. A line
that made us both gasp at the supply spot — "No loneliness is small"

M. chants it all through our labours. The flowers in the lines preceding that
revelation obsess me. Pushing dirt onto thinner dirt, I ask how this poet makes
time a hummingbird. The shushing, like Ritsos' lamps, gets drowsy. Arrange,

arrange again, dig with hands and spade, scrape the roots, place, cover
over, pat. Rev the blower to obliterate the quiet in this work, return us
inarticulate. "Bonkers" is the best we have for Ritsos, for our breathless day.

Turns out our bodies aren't tools. "What a way to feel the world,"
M. drops me at the yard. Thank you, Lolo. You dug a hole
for the planting — that may never happen — to find in us: a welcome.

# REVERIE: CANADA POSTIE WINTER PICKET LINE
*by Ron Romanowski*

Long strike and I need a contract in my pocket
Used the old one
           to stuff a pit bull's mouth
where dim vicious
           thought my hand would be
owner stalked all down the street
              "what'd ya do to my dog!"
I'm a postie and what
    if I had
        a contract in my pocket?

Crocuses would spring
        overnight
leaves unfurl the sweet news
     and grass green green —
when I'd be thumbing
     a new contract in my pocket

Quotidian shuffle-mountain
              of mail
flyers upon flyers upon catalogues
*Urgent.*
*Open.*
*Your million dollars is here!*
      scented love letters?
           comforts for the bereaved?
grime-of-day beat home
              but a contract in my pocket

Wind chill would be a bad memory
so what if
    the spring's street sand
           whirlwinds
      (like the Sahara?)
dust bag socks
     baked gritty feet
           like sliding for home plate all day
I'm a postie
    get me a
        new contract in my pocket

## TOOLS — A LITANY
*by Jane Byers*

cuticle clipper    toothbrush
Sawzall    floss
diamond drill    delight
battering ram    fire
tooth chisel    callipers
abalone shell    grindstone
avalanche shovel    harpoon
nebulizer    mandolin
coffee grinder    twine
teaspoon    shoehorn
forbearance    drum
probe    insulin
spanner wrench    clamp
abacus    lemon zester
Zamboni    Q-tip
hematocrit    telegraph
Acheulean hand axe    javelin
spear    ball peen hammer
laughter    trowel
divining rod    digging stick
Lorazepam    dogleg reamer
tail pipe cutter    patience
awl    runcible spoon
stork beak pliers    syringe
cap chisel    impact driver
stubbly nail eater    words
glass cutter    water
speculum    cup
ochre crayon    breath
rabbet plane    walking
eggbeater drill    rock
pencil    steel brush
carbon calculator
logic    charcoal
amitriptyline    string
flat bastard file    broom
spud wrench    wheel
microscope    sieve

## WHAT IF I TOLD YOU
*by Jennifer Wickham*

What if I told you that
"we are the land, and the land is us"
is *not* a metaphor
our DNA is in the trees
and even if we leave,
our bodies mourn this place

We've been torn and uprooted
scattered and broken

but we are STILL HERE

What if I told you that canada wants to kill us

Not just our "Indigenousness"
our ceremonies and languages
our stories, laws, and songs

They want us in the ground

because our spirits are too strong
and they've been trying to steal our land for too long
we've had ENOUGH

and when we stand up, rise up, war cry with our fuckin fists up
it's time to throw down with the crown

They send the army in
because that's the only way they *think* they can win

and what if I told you they moved in
not knowing that my 3-year-old niece had been moved out
because they don't care about our children
Skïy ze' Ye' toh yez
our future matriarch
one more Witsuwit'en bottoming out their bottom line

She is unbreakable

just like her mother, and her mother and her mother
her bloodline is the mountains, rivers, and trees

What if I told you
that we are ALL the answer to our ancestors' prayers
and what if you believed me?

# REMIND ME ONE MORE TIME
*by Moni Brar*

1
Our father
just out of reach
in the frame of the photo
except his hand on the steering wheel
of his first car, all his fingers still intact.
The photo will make its way to his village
to be passed from hand to hand. They will look
at it in awe: He made it out.

2
Our father is not an architect, nor a carpenter,
framer, builder, or construction worker. He builds
our house in Canada. Divides rooms, tears down
walls, creates new ones. Adds additions
to the additions. Builds a three-car garage
for our one car. Installs a monsoon
in our living room, a jungle in the kitchen.
The floor is sugar canes, the roof bamboo. The walls
neem leaves. Mother watches and disapproves.

3
As the forest fires encroach, we are most worried
about the sunflowers. The thick smoke blocks
the sun. The golden heads droop, look down
and to the sides, unable to locate the sun. We use
our hands to prop up the bee-less heads
of unformed seeds, whisper to them
that the fire will soon abate. We hate ourselves
for telling a big lie.

4
Our brown bodies are bent. We are brown sugar mounds
in the fields that know no time. Our days are anchored
by sunrise and sunset. We pluck fruit,
count our labour in pounds picked. Later,
we learn to replace the word
peasant with farmer, rapeseed with canola.

5
After 84 years of toil, our father dies alone
in a hospital bed. We are on the other side of a blue wall.
We wonder if he remembers the softness of the sun
on his eyelids, the taste of summer on his tongue.

## UN DÍA EN LA VIDA DE UN TRABAJADOR / A DAY IN THE LIFE OF A WORKER
*by Ivan A. Salazar M.*

At dawn, the city yawns,
metallic birds screeching
to the rhythm of a thousand alarms,
coffee stains on worn-out jeans,
he steps out, a ghost among the living.

Concrete jungles stretch their arms,
asphalt rivers flow with noise,
each step a negotiation
with the weight of dreams on his back
and bills that whisper like old friends.

The bus arrives late, as usual,
a metal beast
spitting out the weary
crushed against the glass,
faces blurred, hopes crumpled.

He trades sweat for crumbs,
his hands maps of toil,
calluses tell stories
of a life lived in margins,
where time is currency
and rest is a luxury.

Lunch is a sandwich
shared with pigeons,
who know the art of survival
as they pick at the crumbs
of yesterday's ambitions,
scavenging for meaning.

The sun beats down, a cruel overseer,
yet he smiles at the absurdity
of dreams lodged between subway stops
and the laughter of children
who play in the shadows of skyscrapers.

At dusk he returns
not with riches, but with echoes
of the city's heartbeat,
each horn a reminder
that he belongs to the noise
and the silence that follows.

In the quiet of his room
he counts the day in sighs,
wonders if tomorrow will change
or if the grind will swallow him whole,
yet tomorrow he will rise,
a soldier in the army of the ordinary,
fighting for a life
in the city that never sleeps.

## BEAVER CREEK BUSHWORK
*by Claire Gordon*

Folks out at the Beav
got hit particularly hard
by the bomb cyclone.
Some seriously heinous carnage
out there. I wore sparkly blue
Hunter boots with my bucking pants.
Trudged through limbs,
thorny blackberry vines and bright
rosehips tousled with mud.

The root wad was tacked to three trees.
We limbed them to death
but the jackpot wouldn't spring
back up.
I cut the first tree loose,
made an undercut
into the second cedar's red
cambium and watched it snap.
Two lone stumps
and a depressed alder flung back
to a vertically alive position.

We crossed the creek to investigate
the buildup in the back forty.
Caught a shadowy glimpse of salmon
after spawning, decaying
white-spotted and grey.
They accessed the creek
from the water intake pipe buried
below the logging road nearly
one kilometre upstream.
Swam underground
through the narrow human-made
tunnel and wound up
trapped in the havoc.

Female salmon
will tear their caudal fins
to shreds to generate a redd
and lay eggs. A shiny
full-bodied promise,
slippery focus on creation
at the expense
of all else.

# BUILDING: A PSALM
*by Kurt Armstrong*

Praise the LORD for Monday

Praise him with chirpy alarm and chatty cat;
    with stained and sturdy pants, second-hand shirt,
    coffee, toast, melted butter, thick jam.

Praise with plans and vague ideas, blueprints and napkin sketches,
    with crinkled two-inch photo torn from waiting-room magazine,
    with cut-lists, estimates, deposits, and schedules.

Praise him with profile, contour, and right-angle,
    with bevelled and chamfered edge, pneumatic tools, and compressed air,
    with colour swatches, satin, eggshell, semi-gloss, dead-flat.

Praise the LORD with dust of fibreglass and cellulose,
    with lingering, powder clouds of sanded drywall and drilled concrete,
    with abrasive, caustic grit of smashed plaster.

Praise him with stacks of dimensional spruce and knotty pine;
    with grain and whorl of birch and maple, sweet perfume of sawn fir;
    exotic bubinga, purpleheart, bloodwood, lacewood.

Praise with level joists and plumb studs, sixteen-inch centres,
    with finishing, spiral, ring, box, coated, and galvanized nails,
    with Phillips, Robertson, and Tapcon screws, toggle and lag bolts.

Praise him with leftover pasta, grapefruit, and oatmeal cookies,
    with weariness and a quick lunchtime nap,
    with afternoon coffee run, and half a cookie for the drive home.

Praise the LORD with precision, cabinet doors to a sixty-fourth of an inch;
    praise him, too, when good-enough will pass muster
    because chrissakes, keep moving, we're not building a piano here.

Praise him with demolition and reconstruction,
    with speed square, sliding T-bevel, whirling ten-inch blade,
    quarter-inch round over bit, Olfa knife, and chalk line.

Praise with timbre of hammer drill and oscillating saw,
    baritone drone of huffing dust collector,
    and staccato tattoo of roofing nailer.

Praise him with box joints, blocking, clean cuts, and decent tools,
    with sanded finish, a final coat of mud, and
    if I'm not home by six, go ahead without me.

Praise the LORD with aching lumbar, sweat-stained pits, and stiff wrists,
    with bruised thumbnail, barked knuckles, and dry callouses,
    stubborn slivers, stained fingers, tendonitis, and Advil.

Sing praise to the LORD for hungry, moody kids at the supper table,
    and that I can make use of this body, crackling knee, tender elbows,
    that this haunted mind and frail heart still work.

Praise him with bedtime, old mattress on solid frame, wool blanket,
    with wife-lover-partner-confidant-friend,
    with deep sleep, dreams, predictable two-a.m. piss of the middle-aged.

Praise the LORD for Tuesday

## UNTITLED
*by Kanin Gosbee*

Tip-toe around the soiled root
Fear such that a petal never blooms
Wilted stems who bear only strange fruit

Set without destination
Asymmetrically connected
For all it knows now, the seed is all he ever could be
Seasons like a vinyl record

Younger than the trees, Older than the pages
Wastelands; impregnable and gnashing
If pretty or sweet, Best before

Still, we persist

Another load of laundry
Cycles repeat, But change

Dawn over horizon crest
What lies beyond, forever unknown

Still, we sit patiently and wait for a kiss

Pray you take comfort in the body left behind
Good boys, better man

# WHERE DO YOU SEE YOURSELF IN FIVE YEARS?
by Alison Holliday

you and i both know you aren't really asking me that.
non-newtonian slicked in sunscreen, sweat, and sticky smiles
we both know my hopes and goals fall far behind
my work ethic in regards to its importance to you.
i can make myself the perfect little labourer for an interview:
the one whose biggest dream is to answer the phone
and make money.

                grasping to fictionalize the image of
waking up to the news             *the hottest day of my life so far.*
marking my calendar              *floods of spring; fire of summer*
making my way to the same job   *hurricanes of autumn; frostbite of winter.*
      — or if I am lucky,   a job managing.

    (maybe in the numbing bliss of database cleanup
     i will forget the soft sunlight of childhood,
     the ease of seasons
     the delicate snow of a winter solstice
     a pink-cheeked kiss. lost in the blink of my lifetime.)

i am pretending i can think five years into the future
without imagining apocalypses
    — worse than the one we are currently living —
i would like to be twenty-two and have hope,
and a voice that is not so bitter at the beginning of my career.

## VOICE
*by Zahra Tootonsab*

at bloor st. east, a man in a BMW flips me off
his arm half wet, screaming, "I can smell you from here"
what is new

some white men fear some
Palestinians and flag
a Muslim's chanting

in the rain, my scent lingered
long before your declaration. from جنس
genus to resurgence
I am the smoke of revolutions to continue
choking you out

there is no coincidence
when we stepped inside the cracks
the streets resided in another form
not as rhetoric but as land
back

"when feeling good becomes evidence of justice's triumph"\*
you drive on carbon-neutral promises
on cops beating protestors
on weapons of mass destruction
on whose triumph? whose feelings

matter
into hands

we wreak
wildfires tired of your bullshit
a student uprising
deepens the fragrance of our skins
salt and water

---

\* Lauren Berlant, "The Subject of True Feeling: Pain, Privacy, and Politics," in *Left Legalism/Left Critique*, eds. Wendy Brown and Janet Halley (Durham: Duke University Press, 2002), 112.

sweat sticks my hijab into the folds
of a banner declaring, "NO CLIMATE JUSTICE ON STOLEN LAND
FROM THIS SOIL TO THE LANDS OF PALESTINE"
where fibres meet, there is remembrance
reckoning, tendrils that root
for us, dearest kin

we can feel
you from here
still breathing your breath — در این صدا
wet earth

# GOOD FENCES
*by Jenna Butler*

i.

Slim picking
of birds this season
made gorgeous by loss: the flicker
hammering its cavity under the eaves;
warbler's filament of song
spiralling unanswered.
From the east field,
I watch pelicans slant gingerly
across the slough,
the vast white semaphore flags
of their wings.

ii.

Summer's baleful air,
late rind of snow
the sole measure against burning.
The boreal's crinoline
a fimbriated ghost.

To the south, marshes
blow sere and saline,
dust clouds pluming for days,
salting the ground where they fall.
We steep in sweat and smoke:
respirators for particulate,
goggles for the ash.

iii.

Scant handful of peas
in the combine hopper;
grasshopper techno-fizz.

iv.

The infestation is biblical:
clear wings, two-stripes, road-dusters
rattling like maracas in the wheat.
Days, we harvest under an ash cloud,
one ear tuned to the radio,
the evacuation alerts.
Nights, boom sprayers troll shelterbelts,
carapaces jetting malathion.

v.

Neighbour at the property line
idles his engine, leans from the cab,
ogles our cartridge masks.
*Get a rig with AC,* he says.
*Good for the smoke, the hot weather.*
*Nothing the right tech can't fix.*
*What a humdinger, this climate bunk!*

*Some people,* he says. Rolls his eyes.
*They'll believe just about anything.*

## BAD KIN
*by Justene Dion-Glowa*

The story of how pathetic the two-leggeds were
when the animals first stumbled upon them and bestowed them with gifts
to ensure their survival
is a long one

   and not one that should be written down.

While not there,
I pine for the days of connectivity with nature.

But I am bad kin —

could I ever be good enough
to align myself with what my ancestors knew
or will my hunts forever come wrapped in cellophane — laid gingerly

     upon a styrofoam resting place?

I can burn all the sage I want.
I will not be in good kinship with Earth.
How could I be?

What will Creator think
   of my car driving and
      Ziploc bags and
         Tupperware

When weighed against my
   beadwork
      and art
         and writing
            and death work
               and youth workshops?

        I don't know that my Creator weighs good and bad.

I will have to hope it is intention that matters.
   For I am rich in that
         and that alone.

# THE WORK OF EXTRAS
*by James Croal Jackson*

To be expendable,
a trick from a box
within a budget —

to walk around
another fake New
York holding a bag —

white crinkles with
the weight of something
fake inside. In LA, rain

is rare and sun is eternally
up before everyone else.
The purpose is to cross

the camera, become a blur
for a short second, not even
a body, but a shape of one —

for hire.

## 911 — THIS IS AN EMERGENCY
*by Renee Cronley*

Communities still bleed
from the last round of cuts
to our departments.

We can't coagulate quickly enough
between 911 callers, police officers,
firefighters, and paramedics
when our count is this low.

Call volumes are rising
like the temperatures
of our longer summers,
and lightning keeps striking
tired, dry litters of deadfall
and everything we rely on
is at the mercy of greedy flames.

When trees and their underbrush burn,
tiny solid and liquid particles spread
and suspend in midair, so every breath
is an invitation to climb our bronchial tree
and make a nest in our alveoli.
They can eat away at our insides
in a way that guilt never can.

Medical oxygen is in high demand
so we have to ration our supply,
and take a match to our conscience,
making the difficult decision
of who will have to go without,
and condemn ourselves to the role
of involuntary moral arsonists.

The phone lines are ablaze with pleas for help
burning millions of hectares from our reach.
It is painful to pick up these calls
    knowing
we are dropping them at the same time.

## A TENDER TALE (FOXTAIL BARLEY)
*by David C. Brydges*

The Golden Arrow work bus leaves
transit hub for Suncor refinery
plant outside Fort McMurray.
Passing a grey shipping container,
gasoline tanker, white trucks,
and a big blue zoom boom.
Industrial landscape
of overwhelming realism
beckons the eye to behave
in strict perception parameters.

I yearn as I head to the place
where I will be earning some
visual story of what is seen
from the dirty mud window.
Temporarily ditch my despair
when in the ditch, treasures of gratitude
sing a joyful simplicity, unburdening a
time prisoner heart as we near
security gates, checkpoint border.
Where nature's pleasures have no home.

# BIOX
*by Kate Siklosi*

I distinctly remember walking
nose upward to the flare,
thinking I was walking on rocks
instead of gravelled bones of gulls,
a char of femurs squawking
under a fireball you can see from space.

    *within hours, 7,500 migrating songbirds incinerated.*

darkened pools blooming with benzene
thickened with invisible organisms
buoyed awake by the babbling intake,
drunk on crude, eating away the bad —
humming their arguments for depleted
layers, exploitation, profit and loss.

    *bugs devour the sludge away from view.*

heat of reactor, lull of cat cracker
in the heat of a thousand suns,
high-boiling-point sour water
flows like trust in the river's belly
heavy bitumen chokes its breath
defects and damage discharged by the barrel.

    *the extent of the leak has yet to be disclosed.*

the orange glow of a good life: pensions and
scholarships and generous salaries paid
at the cost of cancers, death, settlement
payments and everything you could want
and need, generations of blue mornings with
coveralls and a rushed donut, boots trampling.

    *someone's gotta do it.*

and just past this chain link fence,
the water runs clear between the rocks,
sending cadmium, mercury, and polychlorinated
biphenyls slinking into the guts and
wombs of communities next door where
baby girls outnumber boys two to one.

>  *they call it a girl-baby boom.*

all this, while nearby we sponge oil off falcons,
zebra mussels strangle 98-year-old pipelines,
tainted walleye stagger gasblind under
the glassy light of the chemical valley
and we feast quietly on organic gristle
and we ask mercy of the sun.

>  *so they say.*

## THE HORSES STILL NEED FED TODAY
*by Trisia Eddy Woods*

This was the third year in a row we were on high alert.
The third year dwelling on ways to evacuate a herd
of twenty-seven horses, with only two trailers.
Spring had brought more rain than expected,
felt promising. Yet a week in July was spent
watching another small town burn.

We've all heard the stories, barns full of horses meeting
their maddened death. Knowing them like we do, we know
the scorched smell of parched prairie grass set alight
will terrify their senses before we are even aware
of its proximity. Embers easily leaping

along hayfields, exploiting tunnels carved by mice,
the earth becoming a simmer. They will feel
the heat running under their pastures, absorb
it through their hooves. It will inflame
nervous systems primed for adrenalin.

This impending fire churns our stomachs
as we scrutinize the weather. Smoke blows in
one dark, moonless night, an unwanted guest settling
on fence lines, blankets, metal roofs of shelters.
The horses cough, deep in their chests,

their eyes grow weepy with the constant
particulate, gummed at the corners.
Lashes clumped from milky discharge.

We speak in low tones about the changing sky,
about the clouds and their strange formations.
Avoid long days outside despite it being August.
For the third year in a row social media posts
call out offers: *Free trailer rides, just text.*
*We have extra pasture if you need, send a* DM.

We practice the scenario in our minds and hope
the horses all get on the damn trailer when we
need them to. The lake is near enough to think
about turning them loose, should the threat
prove to really come that close, that fast.

We get up in the morning and untie bales grown
last summer, fork them over fences, unwind
the yellow hose from the barn and start the process
of filling troughs. Motes dance, softly filtered
on each long rod of sun permeating the early air.

The horses still need fed today.
They still need water.

# DEEP TISSUE
*by Amanda Donnelly*

What we've forgotten about pain
is that it is only the check engine light at the end of the wire
And while I've tactility enough to feel the direction of your muscle fibres
to dissect you into layers of differing densities without breaking the skin
(with only my fingertips, mind you)
I cannot feel your pain, so when
you ask me to root out the incorporeal
I'll seek instead the subtle shift in your breath's rhythm
Resistance in place of pliability

Glide, compress, lift, bend.
Following the braille of your body's story through
the peaks and valleys of your bony landmarks
Hidden places unsafe for habitation
It's there that the villains of your flesh play tug-of-war with your bones
Joints boarded up like derelict buildings
and sinewy contractures sewn by repetition
designed to move and ruined through idling
Another mechanical marvel in disrepair

## BLUE COLLAR MEMORIES
*by Duncan Mercredi*

he carries with pride the scars that have never faded
criss crossing his gnarled hands
he walks with purpose
although the weight of labour has bent his back
he stumbles when he walks
his memories have drifted away
he wakes up some mornings
hands screaming in pain
runs them under hot water
to straighten the fingers
looks in the mirror
searching for who he once was
hair has faded from black to white
telltale lines on his face have aged him
he listens and only hears
the sound of chainsaws and rock drills
that shook his body
he recalls each one horse town he stayed in
a stranger to strangers he avoided
those sleepy villages he travelled through
voices familiar
barking memories
a stranger to strangers
whose names he once knew
he carries with pride the scars that have never faded
the invisible ones stay hidden
the ones he carries to remind him
that the only thing that changes
are the years
my hands hurt

## RISE, GET ORGANIZED
*by Levy Abad*

In the first ten minutes you wrap enough bread
For the boss to pay your daily wage
And you wonder where the rest of the work hours went
On your way home tired and drained

In spite of the wealth that your labours create
Your life's on the brink of falling into a pit
And the harder you work the deeper you sink
While the boss man wallows in wealth

Oppressed you are and mired in precarity
The wealth you made bought your boss's Lamborghini
While the super and lead hand think you're lazy
When you question the system and want to be free

You stare at the conveyors moving at speed
Carrying loads of profit, power, prestige
While what you're paid is just enough for the day
So, in pain, tomorrow you'll be back and you'll stay

All these millions in food that you're packing
You're barely allowed a bit to take home
With a little defect all thrown into the garbage
While working people are starved to the bone

Who stole all the gold that you dug from the mines?
Or the swords and guns that you made with calloused hands?
And for your yearning for freedom, justice, and peace
Who will fire you to starve you or send you to jail?

So rise and liberate your hammered body and mind
And let the greedy tremble with solidarity's might
From workplace oppression, justice and equality are forged
To win and build a new world

# THE SONG OF THE INVASIVE VEGETATION MANAGEMENT TECHNICIAN
*by Ray Owen*

The mullein grows as tall and wide as two of us combined
And the more the goat's beard's taken seed, the less of it you'll find.
Oxeye daisy's pretty, but will fuck a creek bed up
And don't forget the difference 'tween the types of buttercup.

There's overtime past hour ten and hour forty-four;
I swear once summer's over, I shall do this shit no more.

There's many kinds of thistle, and most of them we spray
But I'll take pulling thistle over hawkweed any day.
And under pain of instant death, don't touch the columbine
Or planted trees, or fancy moss — but I forget which kind.

There's overtime past hour ten and hour forty-four;
I swear once summer's over, I shall do this shit no more.

In May and June, the right-of-way's aswarm with sows and cubs —
The grizzly, black, and toothy kind, with paws like bladed clubs.
By mid-July, the baking ground is belching $H_2S$
And UV rays and wildfire smoke make Hell of all the rest.

I'm swimming in my coveralls, their seams are crusted white
And it's been too hot to sleep this week 'til very late at night
But up I get at four a.m.; my debts won't pay themselves —
So here's my mantra, splattered blue — may it comfort you as well:

There's overtime past hour ten and hour forty-four,
I swear once summer's over, I shall do this shit no more.

# ROOING FLEECE
*by SJ Jones and Samantha F. Jones*

i. An average year

   part pull
   the break, a release,
   the wool harvest.

   pick


       pick      pick


pick


       pick     pick

pick
          pick

 pick

pick   it's time
  to lay    pick

    pick in the
           field

and  pick
   pick    pick
  pick
\*\*\*\*\*\*\*\*\*\*\*\*\*\*\*\*\*\*\*\*\*\*\*\*\*\*\*
thrown fleece as the sheep
are ready.

ii. A hot year

    part pull, too late,
    the break: static
    the heat: early

    pick


          pick        pick


pick


          pick     pick

pick
              pick

  pick


pick    it's time
\*\*\*\*\*\*\*\*\*\*\*\*\*\*\*\*\*\*\*\*\*\*\*\*\*\*\*
as soon as the shearer
is available.

## WASTE NOT
*by Judy Parceaud*

Born in London during World War Two
Composting, using everything available
Not a choice but a way of life
Allotments gave us basic veggies
Chickens gave us eggs, then meat
Everything compostable returned to the garden

My father, a research chemist, worked full-time
Creating fire-fighting equipment
For London, being bombed incessantly
Working hard to feed his family

A few years after the war my parents purchased
The house I grew to call home
Further from my father's work
Fuel rationing obliged him to cycle
Twenty miles morning and evening

A three-acre garden
The main attraction
And a rambling derelict house
At seven I was ecstatic
A little garden of my own

Working hard to improve neglected land
He dug a trench across the garden
It seemed so long and why?
Every little scrap of food and weed
Gathered then deposited in the trench
To be covered with soil, forming a new trench

Water was rationed
Baths taken successively
Little ones first then up through the family
Dad took the last bath, relishing his time
Alone in the bathtub, the fifth in that water

Clothes were passed down
Mended as needed but rarely discarded
Hand-knitted sweaters unravelled
New sweaters emerging from old yarn
Toes removed from shoes
Making room for growing feet

How could I forget those habits
Engraved in my young mind
Lasting a lifetime
Kitchen debris in the compost
Old clothes handed down
Or made into something new

For many years I was considered eccentric
Now it's routine for many friends and family
But as I see the chaos of war in the world
I wonder if my little efforts are not futile
Years of care erased overnight with one bomb.

## CLIMATE ACTION IS MY RETIREMENT JOB
*by Jean Clipsham*

Old ladies go through life unseen.
We can get away with lots.
I wonder if this force is green,
Creating climate-movement plots?

We can get away with lots,
'Cause raging grannies are so cute.
Creating climate-movement plots?
Beneath grey hair we are astute.

Raging grannies are so cute.
Are we seeing any shift?
Beneath grey hair we are astute.
Some climate action is what we wish.

Are we seeing any shift?
Stealthiness seems so futile,
Some climate action is what we wish.
Yet our measures are on trial.

Stealthiness seems so futile.
I wonder if this force is green?
Yet our measures are on trial.
Old ladies go through life unseen.

## NECHAKO (2000)
*by Ella Soper*

The mess tent pitches, its doors
loosened from their mooring by the evening's sighs.
Its flaps snap intermittently,
their rigging aloft, bidding darkness and wind welcome.

Gusts, sweetened by the mountain's top,
carry on their backs laughter, loud complaint,
the inevitable chock! chock! of firewood being hewn.

Outside a small colony loosely huddles against twilight
in the cold furrow of the valley —

Each tent bears down on its allotment of unforgiving earth.
Stones, taut guy lines and shovels secure blue tarps
that glow from within, tenacious and unearthly.

Darkness descends like a blow.
Each hillock of humanity defies the snuffing
in this wrinkle of the mountain's hide.
Each camp stranded as are stars in the abandon of sky.

As above, so below —
one man's shirt a constellation,
a galaxy of bloodspray —
the sneezed detritus of a day's labour on the planting block,
where pesticides and altitude conspire to sicken.

Noonsun stays high and long, despite
helicopter blades that streak the sky dusky with brushsmoke
and stir the embers of the pulp mill's sour breath.

## SERVING LA BARRIERE PARK
*by Mike Bagamery*

After we arrive at the park on the southwest edge of Winnipeg,
    we bound across the lawn to the La Salle River.
Make for the footbridge.
Bong, creak,
    bong, creak,
        *bong, creak,*
            *bong, creak,*
                **bong**:
the bridge is showing its age.

This will be a good place to take people on the BioBlitz next week.
Maybe it will inspire them to adopt a park for their project.
When they do, I'll be there for them,
    the supportive coordinator who shares biological information,
    the one who gets them the tools for doing the work,
    a gardener in my own right,
    who nurtures the seeds of ability and curiosity
    they all carry.

My bare head swivels to take in the plants and I think
*Thank goodness for iNaturalist.*
With the push of a button I can capture sound,
    render light, colour, and shape in megapixels,
        the better to contribute to the human project of bettering our home
        through citizen science.

Look ahead, $^{up,}_{down}$ behind, into the woods off the path.
I hope to see no small number of native species.
My ears are perked for the sounds of birds,
    making themselves known through their own words,
    and mammals too.
No snakes are expected:
    this isn't Narcisse.

I practise my photography.
I know Eastern Grey Squirrels well.
They don't want their pictures taken.
They could almost blend into the tree trunks
    except for their rusty faces and snowy bellies.

They dance up and down the trees, the pillars of their lives,
    anchored to each by the grooves in the bark.
I'm sure the squirrels are grateful for that.

Bur Oak, that's a native tree.
So is Eastern Cottonwood.
Until just a few weeks ago,
    I didn't know exactly twenty-four species of trees were native to Manitoba.
Blue Spruce is common here;
    I learn only later that it was introduced,
    but it fits in by looking like the homegrown hero the White Spruce.

Wait, that's a thing we shouldn't have:
    Common Burdock.
Here in Manitoba it is one weed
    that doesn't make too much of a wall for other life;
    it doesn't poke you,
    it doesn't keep everything else from breathing,
    it doesn't rub its creep in your face.

Wait again — on the open eastern edge adjoining the farm, there is a poker:
    European Buckthorn.
    It puts its own chemicals into the soil,
    making it harder for other plants to grow
    and making the climate crisis that much nastier in southern Manitoba.
I feel it with the tip of my thumb and I wince.

*Snap!* Buckthorn, I'll be back for you
    even if I have to get knee-deep in snow
    and can only put pink flagging tape on you,
    so someone else can see you for what you are,
    so they can take you out of the ground.

## ENDURING SYMBOLS OF DISPOSABILITY
*by Kristian Enright*

*You must change your life.*
—Rilke

We who worked at the movie theatre felt inept
when aware of all the waste we accrued:
docile postmodern sculptures left
in the fantastic whimsical living room
of our theatre — just cups and straws bereft

Of most kinds of ritual. Prior to setting
the projector on, we would rush in
to make a semblance of respectability
— quickly — so they would not detect our agility

As they filed in: potential critics to-be
in the endless cycles of consumption
and alleviation — as if simple abstractions.
But there's somehow material sating indelibly …

Behind the screen was an actual chasm
where all the garbage went; we served
a devilish parody, inert matter cast
down to a deeper death than deserved.

Many made things ought to be a toy forever:
my job was in downtown Winnipeg near the university
but was there to make people forget whatever
consequence existed, except catharsis's pity

Perhaps. And yet, as if it were my job
I would imagine an Odyssey of each
object, as if tracking its exile to breach
the boundaries of comfort zones — odd

To consider that of deserted items
the holy grail cup was the one taken
by someone who wished its reuse even
if "convenience" did give it to them.

How many jobs hide things like this?
If the material were only to be recycled,
the very gold of capitalism is pissed
away as if in indifference rendered in icicles.

And when someone would clean the urinals
we sensed capitalism's possible rust
intelligibly; to be young and enthralled
with facing the future not being an eroded bust

Taken fully, as with Rilke's headless sculpture —
of awareness, "there is no place that does not see you"
as if we were remaking earth in gassy pollution: a star
as all half-used satellites revolve around its dying blue.
Unlike sensing a plot hole in a movie, gravity is the future.

We could be among those who ended
the one-use-plastic age to regain the symbols
of sustainability, the word that has tended
the black sheep activist's pastoral
as if we worked in soot of times industrial.

Here, in our theatre, I saw a documentary
on the huge latent surrender-flag screen
that made me join an eco-group immediately
— a job that seemed exiled from movie scenes
and would inspire me towards an ecological re-entry.

## A DIFFERENT KIND OF SUMMER
*by Jennifer deGroot*

It wasn't the broken ankle or the extra demands of the off-farm job.
It wasn't the dead mama and her hungry lambs.
It wasn't the volunteers from all over the world who suddenly wanted to come.

It was the rain.
And the flowers.

For weeks, no months, every time it rained I thought,
"This is probably it for the season.
We've mulched and have not so many sheep and we'll probably be okay.
We'll get a harvest. We'll eat."

But it rained again,
gently.
And more.
And again.

And the grass grew. And still grew.
And the flowers bloomed.
And kept blooming, even when it did stop raining, for a time.

The sun shone warm and gentle.
The rain landed gently.
The trees grew.
The gardens grew.

And the flowers bloomed.

## GAS STATION
*by Caitlin McCullam-Arnal*

fragrant
diesel

growls

extreme cold warning

billows

grey

against the night

my cheeks are
red

tight

my lip corners
raw

old work idles

oil

men who might
never respect me

yet i don't mind

even smile

now that
i
found

my bones

# PEASANT URBANITE
*by Sanita Fejzić*

*Almost everywhere the sound of the human will.*
—Marie Howe

Since the fires in Australia killed three billion animals —
Since the Western Black Rhino grazes on imaginary grasses —
Since like coral reefs Bosnian peasants are on the verge of extinction:
    my grandmothers gone, their husbands too
        our ancestral land sold, its gardens and wells the stuff of story —
Since I am first in my family born in a city —
    first never to have milked a cow
        never to have heard the cock's cocorico, crack of dawn
Since not all Apples or Blackberries grow on trees —
Since the world wide web colonizes the wood wide web
    and the temperature dangerously rises —

Since I planted strawberries and tomatoes in terra cotta pots on my balcony
    I have been as if expecting —
  hands bursting with activity:
      watering, clipping, harvesting, cutting, cooking
          dreaming of edible wilder living —
      permaculture backyard, a tiny writing cabin
            plum trees as in my Nena's orchard in Višegrad
                swings hanging off branches —
  dreams of grapevines cascading, water-swollen
        shading my face as I stretch to the heavens
           to pick the earth's candy —

Since my soles touched soil unmediated and I dared to dwell in that grief —
Since I looked in the mirror and saw the urban monstrosity —
    how I was conditioned and seduced —
        how I craved more like an anxious lover —

Since I decided to plant the seeds of peasant futurisms
    here, in this poem —
        there, in my urban yard —
          every syllable a society of worms regenerating
  the desertified soil of mind
        the mercury, lead, and arsenic in the backyard —

Since on our table
  a bowl of tomatoes and strawberries —

As an era ends —
as beginnings germinate —
I, peasant urbanite, plant, write, plant, write.

## NO
by Dani Spinosa

*—for Sam Bernstein*

## IN VANCOUVER
*by Leah McInnis*

sitting outside t&t supermarket
the day my family left ft mac
may 3, 2016
working at a yaletown gallery
then going to east pender studio
losing keys
avoiding a birthday dinner
tall can on commercial
losing my mind
going to studio at 6 a.m. to get keys
and i got in trouble in the meeting
because i was wearing my studio clothes to the gallery
but i worked on the top floor
no one saw me
except for that man
who wandered up and said *i want a painting that looks like this*
and i said *i can make it for you*
and the gallery stepped in
and took their cut
and they wrote a press release saying
my painting was influenced by the fires
and maybe it was
but i was influenced by money
i think
more than anything
and a better one could be
phone numbers spray painted on horses let loose
old man on mountain bike with stick in hand and shirt tied around face
dog ashes in purse at the italian restaurant

## DUE DILIGENCE IS NO DEFENCE
*by Lisa Mulrooney*

Who is the god of oil and gas?
a redneck politician / a CEO / my husband
his boss

Who is the goddess?
a preacher's wife / my sister-in-law / me
my alter-ego

    I don't know anymore.

Loyalties and petty jealousies are lanced
hurled like thunderbolts
into the land of mortals

Disciples (personhood devoured)
tell tales of reclamation
    the beauty of fracking
    sweet distance
    drought-hardy alfalfa saving us from low yield outcomes

I love this land as much as the next person
but who is the next person?
my daughter / my son

    I don't know anymore.

The earth itself sends smoke signals
from the pristine prairie it remembers

In Redcliff, the hills across from the South Saskatchewan River
are steaming; the coal still burns, angry
while houses collapse into tunnels
left behind by the miners

We are a singular humanity
embracing these burdens, chasing
herds of white-tailed deer
surrender-flagged, away
from the tailings ponds where
    1600 ducks died at Mildred Lake
    the year my daughter was born

Pumpjacks, Pan-like
are not the only cloven-hoofed spectacles
on this acidic land

Dams break and we cannot mix
the baby formula
we cannot bathe the children

Still, we pray
    to the gods and goddesses we think will save us
    to a last race of deities

    I don't know anymore.

Lighting flare stacks instead of incense
ignoring the rotten-egg smell of hydrogen sulphide
    we forget we are in this together
    souring, indignant
    innocent, unborn

## MOTHBALLING MOULD BAY, NWT
*by Kelly Shepherd*

This was my job: to operate the massive pump that shot the diesel fuel into the air, and the massive torch that ignited it. Behind this torch, which was like a piece of artillery, was a small portable trailer with side-by-side windows and matching easy chairs for two of us to sit in and watch the flame. This was my office.

Two guys on twelve-hour night shift, two guys on day. Not that night or day mattered because this far north in July it never got dark.

The torch needed constant attention: the diesel had to burn clean, and there were environmental consultants around to ensure that it did. If there was smoke, I tweaked the compressor just a little, enough to make the flame hotter. A thunderous twenty-foot jet of flame, twenty-four hours a day for two weeks straight. It was windy on the island, and we couldn't let the flame blow out.

Mould Bay is a joint Canada-US Cold War-era weather station on Prince Patrick Island, in the Northwest Territories. Used to be staffed year-round by something like twenty people, but now a little computer or robot or something does all the work here that needs to be done.

When humans closed the place up, they didn't take much back with them. To this day the rec room still has a pool table and a piano. The library is still full of books. There are dormitories, kitchens, and workshops that look almost occupied. Slowly gathering polar desert dust. There are old vehicles parked here and there, and big military-green generators rusting outside. Once it was considered reasonable to bring these things up here by ship; now it would be far too expensive to think about bringing any of it back.

Our foreman was a grizzled old-timer who had been all over the North and brought with him a battered guitar and a bottle of spiced rum. He said to me, *You go ahead and take some of these books. They're just going to sit here and rot. See those big tanks? It would cost a lot more to ship all this diesel fuel out of here than it's actually worth. But we can't leave it here! Dangerous as hell that it's been sitting as long as it has. When these tanks rust through the spill will be incredible. We have to get rid of it.*

*We're going to burn it.*

## FIRE SEASON
*by Jessica Smithies*

The phone is ringing
Wind is on the other line
His house is burning

The phone is ringing
She doesn't know what to do
"Where do I go now?"

The phone is ringing
Interactive fire maps
Saved to my desktop

The phone is ringing
Coworkers scared for family
Smoke burning my nose

The phone is ringing
Burning question on their minds
Is this covered?

The phone is ringing
They're telling me to stay strong
Tears fall to my cheeks

The phone is ringing

# BITUMEN REFINING AND ITS OUTCOMES: A SHORT COURSE
*by Ross Belot*

\*

deeply discounted, high nitrogen,
high sulphur, high heavy metals,
high naphthenic acid, high filterable
solids, Claus unit filling up,
desalter burping rag layer of
water-oil-and-solids emulsion,
metal pipes thinning, eaten
by complex mixture of cycloaliphatic
carboxylic acids & plain old
aliphatic sulphurs

\*

We loved it because it was hard. They loved us running it because they could place equity production with us. We loved our equipment. We did what was needed. We pushed our equipment to its limits with the worst oil the Earth could offer up. And then we ran some more. We didn't care how they got it out of the ground. We were heroes.

\*

*Naphthenic acid corrosion is often localized, leading to pitting and grooving in metal surfaces like pipes, which can create holes resembling Swiss cheese. This is especially problematic in areas with high fluid velocity or turbulence, where the corrosive effects are amplified*

run even more of this stuff they said & we did,
hexavalent chromium corrosion inhibitors,
metalled up the big atmospheric
and vacuum distillation units with
chromium, nickel, molybdenum, ever
more expensive alloys, we ran
feasibly, inspected metal thicknesses
regularly to avoid catastrophic failure,
so like they asked we ran the hardest stuff

\*

*Certain types of solids can act as surfactants, migrating to the oil-water interface and stabilizing emulsion.*

We did what we could and sometimes had to cut the nasty crudes out and go back to plain vanilla crudes. That was failure, we were not loved. You couldn't predict. They could take the bitumen out of the sand, but they couldn't take all the sand out of the bitumen. The oil-coated solids would form emulsions and carry under in the desalter brine and overwhelm our water-treatment facilities. It was not good.

\*

> the bitumen came 2600 kilometres,
> along the way it came through
> breakout tanks mixed with other crudes,
> sometimes tanks along the way had sludge,
> sometimes they didn't,
> sometimes tanks' mixers were working.
> sometimes they weren't,
> it came and we didn't know
> what we were going to get,
> sometimes we dealt with it,
> sometimes we couldn't

\*

On the plane coming back from Calgary's Conference for Running Challenged Crudes someone said to me "You might want to read this …"

*Pikas with nowhere to go — too hot below, too hot where they are due to climate change. Moving further up until they run out of mountain —*

\*

Many of us retired. We didn't get told any more that we were heroes. We didn't get told any more "way to go!" Many of us mostly played golf.

\*

I went to California, found myself
reading poems to refineries, went
on Refinery Healing Walks
organized by Idle No More SF Bay,
heard Indigenous leaders say the oil
wasn't to blame for climate catastrophe,
the oil belonged to the Earth
that we had ripped it from,
we were the ones doing violence,
we were not heroes, I watched
California burn, watched the sky
turn grey and red for days, acrid
smoke stung my eyes, acrid smoke
hurt my lungs

*

## ROOFER
*by Sabrina Spenser Smith*

The world is burning and you couldn't catch Roofer
dead with a mask on. Two stories up, he inhales

the sky into his tar bags and spits a loogie
full of forest. Roofer is another way of saying shit

out of luck. The reason Roofer pisses so freely
in backyards is because he's always putting out

fires. Nails for breakfast and yet here he is
breathing. It's a miracle, really, and when song

is the next thing from his mouth — Great Balls
of Fire and then some old Taylor Swift

number — the great flood comes again
and Roofer floats away on his roof.

## 988
*by Fiona Conway*

what words do I have for the child, 13, on the phone
telling me she wishes
her parents had never
had a child
telling me she is
so afraid of the way
her breath warms the world

## CARBON OFFSETS
*by Rina Garcia Chua*

Maybe a single breath
inside a compressed
cabin wastes a litre of oil.

Is it possible to go without?

If only tears shed from takeoff
to touchdown could be an engine
that connects continents.

I have cried a million barrels —

I could scoop them up without
dropping any into the ocean
and offer them to the fuselage.

There is so much more in me —

until I have crossed six thousand
miles, until my breaths have merged
with your tiny, powerful ones.

Is it possible not to go without?

## SWELTERING COLLEGE CLASSROOMS
*by Catherine Parceaud*

High windows along two walls
sunshine streaming in
leaving bright patches
of light on desks

My smile greets thirty-two students
spilling into class
we get rolling
introductions and course outline

Our classroom heats up
human bodies shifting about
clustered in this enclosed space
focus wavers

Heat is palpable
like a weighted blanket applying pressure
molding itself around our shapes
air suspended in place

Eyes start glazing over
ok, now we're sweltering
let's open the door
get air circulating

Wishful thinking
doesn't make much difference
noise in hallway
close door again

Our minds overheating
the warmth drains students of their drive
melting away in puddles
that evaporate at their feet

Finally, we are done
"See you next week!"
students hurry out of class
leaving heated air behind along
with lingering odours of perspiration

With a long sigh I erase the whiteboard
exit classroom into stale hallway
year after year, it gets worse
hotter for longer
there's no going back

## WIININAAMOWIN, AIR POLLUTION
*by Renée E. Mazinegiizhigoo-kwe Bédard*

in my ancestors'
office was a lodge
the floors were
lined with cedar
the walls birch bark
sweet vanilla scent
of hanging sweetgrass braids
cattail mats were
scattered about the floor
their office was nature
their conference room
was along the river
surrounded by forest
they went to work
along a trail
scattered with plant
medicines and wildflowers
rabbits, eagles, and bears
were their colleagues
air smelling of pine needles
warmed by the sun
filled their nostrils
carpets were moss
laid under their feet
their office floors
were dark black earth
teeming with life
the walls were blue skies
and green swaths of leaves

my ancestors' office
looked different
than mine does
in my office
the floors are
synthetic carpet
plastic everywhere
nothing is natural
the walls are painted beige

my desk is
particle board and laminate
i have some windows!
that's a bonus!
plants in pots
cover my metal filing cabinet
the air is recycled
i burn sage
to clean the air
to feed my spirit
the air is dead
and dying in buildings
where my office is
the air can't move
it is not fed by the trees
my people call that wiininaamowin, pollution
the air was colonized
it got no treaty
who cares about the air?
who takes care of the air?
i do! i do! i care!
i burn sage to decolonize it
to feed the spirit of the air

## INTO THE COULEE
*by Evan Woelk Balzer*

On each month's second Wednesday
From one till three p.m.
I take a Zoom call with a team
That all confronts the end

The lead was there ten years ago
When the pastures were undone
He's watched the birds he's loved so much
Vanish one by one

But still he sends the link each month
He knows us all by name
We form our screen-lit commune there
And play the monthly game

In which new way have we lost hope
And how shall we endure?
Which species stands at precipice
And are we truly sure?

From offices and basement spaces
Twenty people gather
A coalition of the few
To say these grasslands matter

We know that most but not quite all
Will never stand and hear
A pipit's trilling song above
Or bobolink so clear

So as rare birdsong fades from places
Few and far between
We launch our app and pray the gap
Has not yet grown too lean

And as I close that call each time
I think of my own son
For whom I join that Zoom call
For whom this work is done

## BARRY
*by Brad Fougere*

Barry and I met working at a superstore.
He was full of funny quips like
    "Figures don't lie, but liars sure can figure"
and
    "I'm preparing my kids to dig through piles of discarded cellphones
    for unopened relish packets."
He was from an older generation,
    a teenager in the era of acid rain and holes in the ozone layer.
I wanted to organize a union,
but maybe I should be looking at buying a shovel.

## BOOTSTRAPS
### Labour Day, Lordstown, Ohio
*by Jim Daniels*

Myth/legend/Bible verse defining the hell
of purgatory. Theory of turning the other cheek
smacked down by the human limit to cheeks.

Jesus got a gold star in Conduct, but failed
the math of cynicism. Pause for the cause.
Head scratch. Welding spark burning the eye.

Light bulbs improved, but not the ideas.
The wasted wattage of a life? The industrial
heartland got a mechanical valve

in a surgical procedure approved of
by loud musicians in the Cacophony Café.
Time clocks offered no smiley face. Just

literal punching in and out. I knocked
on the door of the vacant factory staring up
at clouded high windows where the overhead

crane once functioned — sideways elevator
for the illusion of mobility. I dreamt the crane
hooked people, not steel rolls — not steel roles.

The myth of *safety* glasses and hearing
*protection*. The smokestacks are giving up
cigarettes forever. Down here, we're learning

how to vape and make playlists of our
greatest hits. The plunge into silent blindness
in the back of the church of the anonymous.

I dreamt we levitated to the factory roof
like in the aerial photo they presented me
as a gift to retire early, shortening the daily

line of ants drawn to the fake sweetener
of the American dream. We carry signs
in the sun, on strike at the abandoned plant,

nostalgic for darker sweat inside the gates,
across the parking lot cracked with old promises
and the latest lies. Nostalgia eats us for lunch,
washes us down with gasoline, while the myth

of wind turbines killing any flying thing lingers
like microparticles of grease beneath the nails
and fingernails and behind the ears, perfumed.

Wasn't it great, brother sister dad uncle aunt
grandpa? Plenty of time now for ethnic dancing,
ritual exorcisms, singing lessons, fire drills.
All those years of taking it

of taking it     taking it     taking it
a living         a living       a living
and so, those who oversimplify overcooked

the crow, and so, we gobbled it up, believing
our acceptance would pay off. I don't know
how, peering through the blackened eye

of the telescope joke. Everything distant,
the graffiti of our votes turned into con-fetti
in the great American tradition.

So, why do my hands tremble as I write
one more cheque to myself, overdrawn forever
in the land
          of good
                   behaviour?

# WORK    WORDS    WORK

—after "Work Body Work" by Julie Paul in Whiny Baby

by Marjorie Poor

| WORK | WORDS | WORK |
|---|---|---|
| I work with | words | at work I |
| fix work of | others I | edit I change |
| | | |
| at work I can't | trust anything | (least of all my |
| memory) look up | spellings look up | facts look up |
| | | |
| references I | look for | missing commas |
| missing periods | missing words | I look for |
| | | |
| misplaced commas | misplaced colons | misplaced words |
| I look for | misused words | misused commas |
| | | |
| misused ellipses | I judge | at work and I |
| find the work | of others | wanting I remove |
| | | |
| nonsense at work | I substitute | *learner* for |
| *student* I change | *comprised of* | to *composed of* |
| | | |
| *utilize* to *use* | I add *the following* | so the colon |
| (they insist on) | is correct I add | parentheses |
| | | |
| so abbreviations | like *etc.* | fit our style guide |
| I change hyphens | to en dashes | to mean "to" or to |
| | | |
| make super-hyphens I | change hyphens | to em dashes |
| make bulleted | lists parallel I remove | extra spaces between |
| | | |
| sentences I remove | scare quotes around | ordinary words |
| at work I argue | about whether | facts can be |
| | | |
| created about | whether documents | need to be |
| socialized about | what a sentence | really means |
| | | |
| about whether we | want to say | something or |
| just make up words | that no one can | understand |
| | | |
| at work I try | to figure out | what is being |
| said but sometimes | it's just | a wild guess |
| | | |
| at work I look | for some kind | of meaning |
| some sort of | vision to work | toward |

## COFFEE CENTRE CALL SHOP
*by Luana Terán*

Colombian
Coffee
Self-fulfilling
Prophecy
But also
No accent
Call centre
Access
Thank you for calling —
Yes welcome. What can I get you —
And there's chlorine in the vents
The rats were looking for a warm place
But there's no open windows
No evacuation
There's Customers on the line
All the same
Outside air stings
Just as much
Last summer was sooo —
Yes welcome. What can I —
I understand your frustration
May I put you on hold —
Call time: 1:03:25
Caramel Latte for John!
Yes the oat milk is —
Thank you for holding —
Sell your jacket
No more snow
I just bought this jacket
There was snow this morning
We had rats this morning
Number of calls: 165
Order number 28 up!
Yes. Hi. How. What. Can I. Help. For calling.

# NICE PEOPLE WEATHER SPEAK
*by Lena Palacios*

In front of the ER
Six hours into a twelve-hour shift
Sweating bullets in the unnatural heat
Nice people interrupt my unnatural smoke break
"For sure you're loving this beautiful weather, eh?"
My eyes roll into the back of my head unnaturally

Canada Nice
Minnesota Nice
All love weather speak

Complaining about cold in winter
Complaining about heat in summer
Complaining about rotting leaves in fall
Complaining about manure smell in spring

Love to talk seasonal change
Not climate change
Never dead and dying polar bears
Never dead and dying caribou and salmon
Never First Peoples prevented from hunting
On their traditional unceded lands
Dead and dying due to
Nice people

Or murdered Black people by cops
Or murdered Indigenous kids
By farmers with guns
Or Brown babies blown up
By overseas empires led by
Nice people

In the Fall
The leaves have pretty colours
Nice people say

But even the falling leaves cannot stand
Nice people weather speak
They and the birds prefer suicide

Drifting, slamming
Earthward bound, anything but
Smell skyward wafting stench of
Pumpkin Spice Chai Lattes
Nice people chemical warfare

Canada Nice
Minnesota Nice
All love weather speak

I go back to work in
Bloody triage rooms
Back to nursing refugees of
Climate crises
Corporate injustice
COVID-19 hellfire
Geopolitical racism
Medical disparities
Nice people, no end

No translators on floor
No fucking PPE left
Anti-union asshole admin
Doctors with borders
Without boundaries
Coffee machine broke
Out of cancer sticks and

All my unnaturally nice supervisor can say
In Canada Nice weather speak
"For sure you're loving this beautiful weather, eh?"

Canada Nice
Minnesota Nice
All love weather speak

## AN ENERGY-CONSCIOUS WORKPLACE
*by Bonnie Quan Symons*

Since COVID,
our offices became more energy conscious.

Our photocopiers are on "standby."
They only turn on when staff walk by,
or stand in front of them.

Our water-dispensing coolers
replaced the previous heavy jugs of delivered bottled water.

Floor by floor,
our washrooms were renovated —
automatic flush toilets,
sensor-activated soap dispensers
and faucets.

On one day each June,
we have *Purge Day* —

no work meetings can be held that day.

Paper documents get shredded,
emails and electronic files are deleted.
Dead batteries, used computers, electronics
are dropped off to be recycled offsite.

There are two daily prize draws,
the first in the morning,
a second in the afternoon.

Also, a prize gets awarded to the person
who deletes the most emails!

# WE SLEEP WITH THE WINDOWS CLOSED
*by Yolanda Hansen*

The first night of baby's cold, I dozed in the nursery recliner,
his wheezing a slow accordion in the midnight silence.
I dreamed of lungs as pink as kitten noses,
red like the inner shell of a rabbit's ear.

Nothing prepared me for motherhood's fox ears,
attention pricking to each snuffle, snort, sigh,
the assault of noise as baby grew and filled
crystalline air with squeals in the lush summer backyard,

singing to the car radio, windows rolled down
in the golden hour, laughter on an August beach. Rainy days
used to be the only thing keeping him home
from the lake, now his mouth forms words

like Air Quality Index, wildfire smoke, particulate matter,
the worst fire season on record, the new normal.
Each cancelled sport practice, delayed outdoor party
draws protestations, settles into disappointed huffs.

A summer cough is a dart to my ears and I dream of dark smoke fingers
grasping orange sky. We sleep with the windows closed
and before bed, I linger at his open door, straining for the puffs
of his breath above the rabbit thump of my heart.

# THE ADVOCATE
*by Ikeoluwapo B. Baruwa*

I step into offices
Scan laboratories
Walk the worn paths of classrooms and halls
Each step whispers a question
What risk waits here?

Slips, falls, unseen dangers
I trace them back to their roots
Chemicals stored in shadowed corners
Paper-thin walls guarding against a storm

Your lecture halls ring with knowledge
But I come before the echo
Ensuring the air is clean enough to fill your lungs
I stand behind the glass of a lab bench
Watching for hazards that don't just break bones
But leach into rivers, into skies, into futures

I do this because you deserve more
Because I know life doesn't hand out safety
Because the storms outside
The floodwaters, the rising heat
Are not just nature's chaos

Each hazard I find is a reminder
We build the risks we face
But in the building
There is hope for *unbuilding*, too

## CLOSING SHIFT — 2525 MAIN ST. — 11/9/2020
*by Olivia Ingram*

from behind the counter on the SW corner of Main and Broadway
I see the sky is a boring dolour, accented by crows

the twilight horizon cut short by high rises,
their seemingly unstoppable neon reflected in slick-down blacktop,

and the scarcity of people anywhere on the street
makes eerie the atmosphere of the once-busy corridor

all refracted through Kafka's windows — the cafe, not the author;
however ironic, however fitting, the latter —

where they'll drink coffee and hum anti-war ballads with catchy choruses
of dead students and failed revolution,

to the tune of scarcely living wages,
where we will not be recognized as essential workers, yet clearly are

where they'll misrecognize *for what it's worth*
to forego safety and solidarity for a cup of normalcy,

while we stuff manila bags with pistachio financiers and tired arguments
of repression and disaster and lipstick stains on diner mugs.

and when it's all over,
alone in an empty cafe,

I'll take my mask off and stand at the end of the counter
to drink the last espresso of the day

and remember Roethke's lines about work and desolation in public spaces
in the silence of a mouse

dying sharply on a trap under the faulty refrigerator

like so many creatures in the city
at this time in our present catastrophe

# CLIMATE ADVERSITY
*by Lance Guilbault*

I taught students today
The fire surrounded us
We could feel the heat
As the sweat dripped
From foreheads to feet
They continued to write

We sat in the school
As the tornado
Ripped at the roof
And pulled our
Emotional heart strings
They continued to read

Climate change article was read
Highlighters in action
Spilling across the page
Just as the pipeline
Spills across the sage
They continued to learn

Despite the torrential waters
Raining down from
The waskoya (clouds)
Their moccasins filled
They continued to think

The drought dried the air
As the faucets dripped
Topsoil windstorm
Pelted the glass panes
Blasting an unknown rhythm
They continued to study

They worry of a future
Learning, reading, writing,
About the exploitation
Of the land, the water
Anything we can touch
They asked how come they don't learn?

A question I cannot answer

## BE A SECURITY PROFESSIONAL
*by Martin Durkin*

You are

the no fun police
fake police

Standing (12-hour shift)
Walking (3 miles per hour)
Invisible (in a bright yellow reflective vest)

A clown from a movie
who falls asleep
feet up on the desk
while robbers prowl on the CCTV

The script says
security is not a real job
to take seriously

So

if you do

God protect you at 3 a.m.
or 7 p.m.

While you patrol outdoors in
whatever weather
Mother Nature sends
next shift

Be the mall guard prepared
for another
mother

who drops off her
12-year-old
saying

Her abandoned angel
could never ...

While you're on radio
calling in the
ready-to-go-home guard
from outside
to assist.

# I STRAP THE SUIT ON
*by Rob Madden*

ventilator a rib over helmet,
scuffed visor a blurred screen
torso fastened with clamps to arms and legs.

I pull hose from compressor, adjust the nozzle
and blast concrete between boots.
the draw from the machine makes it
disturbed and unstable, rocking
back and forth on the blocks.

it hisses through hands
and seams the sidewalk in bursts.
the machine arcs in that humped noise,
ramps up a long complaint of pistons and air
a rushed racket that kicks up from the effort

to keep it focused, continuous,
to keep it from falling apart.

this is what it does.
this is what I do.
obliterate something to keep something else
from falling apart.

I wear down parts.
I stay on task.

the sound of it in the air around the suit, around me
blasted in the exhaust of this machine.

a hurtled wheeze.
a dragged rope flung under the early morning

blue-black dome
this sky has already become.

## PROFESSIONAL EXPERIENCE
*by Jessica Bebenek*

everybody alone with their little jobs making their little monies alone in co-working spaces alone at work wearing a blazer alone on an escalator in the eaton centre downtown in montreal or toronto or alone with my resume being interviewed alone as I rock to sleep someone else's child with a man in a blue windbreaker alone on his bike making a buck alone at a café behind the counter or at a table alone with his macbook in the rain walking to work with one hand on the umbrella the other on alone with a customer laying patiently as I press clammy electrodes to her bare chest and wrists and ankles and alone as I sit to roll up my pant cuffs to share my new socks with alone with a tripod with mounted ring light with the whole world as I do my little clapping rolling dance of alone with today's sponsor with something on in the background while I write my little emails alone and remote with a headset taking the call of alone while committed to offering exceptional service because we value the alone you feel while you sit at your desk while I sit at mine alone with the fear of being more afraid to visit the alone the external empty of alone in the cave of alone with the moss and shadows of alone creeping in to fill up the inside walking alone like a monk in saffron robes towards the sea towards the desert towards the mountainous great range of alone

## LEAF-MURMUR
*by Christine Lowther*

You were working your first job fifteen years before an email
said *Print this and tape it to the door.*
Two words: Cooling Station.
And no AC because the premises had been built wisely.
You've been working your second job ten years
in year-round shorts. Temperature control is kilometres away
so you send heat out open windows.
Trees shaded patient rooms, but the trees were felled.
No one asks you what that was like. Or what scares you now.
The heat is out of your hands. The heat is lost out windows.
It's like you are a moving part of the building.
A tool to make computers work.
A tool to disappear the packaging.
Not like you have kidneys that will cook under heat domes.

They want to build a new library.
They want to build a new hospital.
They always want to build new,
with greenhouse glass and remote control. AC and no shade.
Clear away old trees for newness, no creative inclusion,
just replant (during a drought). You will work there.
It is you who must search for someone
who will hear your concerns:
on-site climate command.
Sterilize here, don't ship out.
Recover, restore, and read under trees.
Build around mature trees, close to patient windows.
Use bird collision-proof glass.
Aim the outside lights down.
Heal with biophony, leaf-murmur, and shade.

# DISABLED BY ME/CFS AND LONG COVID
*by M.S. Marquart*

I am mainly alone, housebound in a small studio apartment

I keep the lights off to subdue sensory overload

No flights to visit nieces, parents, in-laws, friends, tourist spots

No travel to shop for throw-away retail therapy

I can seldom shower; it stresses my symptoms and knocks me out

No energy to hand-wash, I save water with full dishwashers

Staying inside, I rarely use energy-consuming outdoor resources

I manage unwanted needs; loved ones support as they can, all of us unpaid

I keep the AC on all summer to calm temperature sensitivity

No walking to buses or subways, each medical visit requires a car

No fresh food, I subsist on disposable snack packs stored next to the sofa

I trash IV bags, tubing, and more waste after monthly nurse visits

As my body fattens, I need new online-thrifted clothes

Orders are shipped to my door, swaddled in plastic packaging

## ISLANDERS PREPARE FOR CATEGORY 4
*by Credell Simeon*

Bear Beryl
Bear her destruction
Bear her isolating disconnection
Tourism stands in traumatic pause
Canadians distraught vacating the islands,
bare.

Bear Beryl
Bear her storming pain
Quick harsh labour
One big rush of air pounding
Birthing us out into the open,
bare.

Bear Beryl
Bear her strength
Cast down in hammering judgement
The warning silent against the winds
Lifting off flying flocks of roofs everywhere,
bare.

Bear Beryl
Bear her sorrow
Grief over eighteen lives lost
Count only one for the earliest record of hit and run
Reckless unstoppable freak tragedy islands,
bare.

Bear Beryl
Bear her swirls
Tornadoes torturing us hopeless
Wood cast out and up like useless words
Damn nails pierced our fate to the cross,
bare.

Bear Beryl
Bear her terrible news
Sister islands in peril
Humanity threatened unapologetically
Run sheep run away to shelter hope fleeting,
bare.

Bear Beryl
Bear her bent branches
Electricity cut lines sparking shock
Despair watered down into emptiness
Tears running in gutters lost to the rough seas,
bare.

Bear Beryl
Bear her arrival
Preparation drowned in fear of her departure
Her incoming surges storm us
Our convictions of faith bottled in empty spirits,
bare.

## THE AFTERMATH
*by Peace Akintade-Oluwagbeye*

According to the western version of individualism,
your root starts with yourself: *id, ego, self.*

You start as a seed, become a tree,
become the leaves, become the sun,
become photosynthesis, become the rain,
the clouds, and the sky.

You become the hemisphere,
the world revolves around you,
the sun revolves around you.
*You* the root, your *id* the leaves,
your *ego* the skies.

If your version of care
becomes corrupted or
the roots start to decay,
the drought starts to stay,
the leaves turn brown.

Who do you turn towards?

Who helps you grow again?

The sky, your *id*.
The moon, your *ego*.
The rocks, your *self.*

Who will you turn to?

*It is not enough for the (b)lack twenty-something to continue to rot in self-isolation.*

The trees think they grew
through willpower and nothing else.

The (b)lack twenty-something
has grown tired of watering plants
that believe life     *came from their own mind.*

Is the (b)lack twenty-something
a concept to those who believe in individualism?

An oak tree reaches
the limits of the hemisphere,
it turns around and
sings praises to mother nature.

For a moment, mother nature smiles.
For a moment, the oak's gratitude cleanses her lone-liness.

## ARCTIC ADORATION
*by Ashley Qilavaq-Savard*

can you imagine just barely escaping a snowstorm
enough to witness it in all its glory at your tail's end
swallowing whole your home like a
sneaky fox and clueless lemming
swiftly, naturally, unapologetically
suffocating and cleansing all in the same
to feel that fierce wind forcing you into the self-realization of resilience
eyes squinting as a million tiny snowflakes dance so elegantly before you
lungs erupting with crisp clean air, heart outpouring the essence of the land
from the most quenching breath, you feel our ancestors flowing through
        your veins
leaving only clarity and vitality as they journey through you

## ORGANIZER'S CAR
*by Alex Gallo-Brown*

The union organizers gather
at the taco truck outside Chevron
alongside workers who labour
outside of their jurisdiction.
*The city is too expensive now,*
one of the workers says
as he ladles salsa
onto potatoes and chorizo,
holding tight to his Mexican-born Coke.
The organizers nod but avoid his eyes.

I toss my tacos
onto the passenger seat,
ignoring the half-empty cup
of coffee in the cupholder
and box of donuts on the floor.
*An organizer's car*, more than one
person has said admiringly,
although I do my best
to clean it.

*In the world I imagine*
is a phrase I read
in a poem once.
*In the world, I imagine*
is a feat I often struggle
to attain.

## HOLD, PLEASE
*by Lia M. Markin*

I sit at my desk.
I wait for the beep.
Another call.
Another voice on the other end
of a wire,
another script to follow,
another promise to make
that I can't keep,
that no one keeps.

The headphones press tight,
muffling the hum of the machines,
the hum of the world beyond
that's slipping further away,
one burning summer at a time.

*Thank you for calling —*
*how can I help you today?*
Say it. Like I mean it.
Like we're not already drowning in the wait,
the endless *hold*
that no one talks about,
where the music plays on,
on loop,
a sweet lie about waiting
for the fix to come.

There's a fire somewhere.
I sniff it in the air,
in the lines we trace between us,
the hold time growing longer
as the storms get louder
outside,
somewhere past the glass doors,
where we forget to look.

*Please hold,*
I repeat,
like I'm giving them time
to catch up,
but I'm the one
catching my breath,
wondering how much longer
I can keep pretending
this is the job I signed up for.

Wondering how much longer
I can ignore the heat
creeping through the cracks,
the quiet, insistent way
the world burns and burns
while we wait.

The call ends,
and another begins.
I type out another fix,
another apology,
another promise I can't keep.
But I don't say the words anymore.
I just wait for the beep
to start the next one.

*Hold.*

## AN INORDINATE NUMBER OF INSECTS (FIELD NOTES FROM A NATURALIST)
by Karen Loucks

The forest is alight,
a strange red brightness
beneath a smoke-sick sky
that chokes on its own bile.

In my mind's eye: mountainsides luxuriant, carpeted
in a costumery of green — sage, chartreuse, emerald.
The gleam of gold that is a grove of larches.

But the trees are sick now, pustules of sap
pockmarking the near-impervious bark
of otherwise healthy trees, beetles
      black, the size of a grain of rice
bore through the tough armour
into soft, spongy phloem
to feast, to deposit eggs.

These are the colonized: *western white pine,*
*whitebark pine, ponderosa pine,*
*lodgepole pine, golden larch,*
*white spruce, Engelmann spruce.*

Thick stands reduced to the fire-end of matchsticks,
drought-finished; this is not a catwalk
of deciduous fall fashion.

I take off my shoes to feel again
beneath my feet the soft duff
that holds water, a kind of safekeeping
like this notebook I clutch —
thirty years memorializing
on waterproof paper
with thixotropic ink
the multitudes
that make a forest.

Take, for example, the rein orchids —
their late-spring race,
thrust of tender shoots,
tiny blooms — tropical beauties
skimming the edges of a yellow-cedar bog,
dancing in the arms of pines
while the forest floor warms, fragrant
with decay and new life.

Or the five-alarm cheep of a pika,
intruder sighted, tiny cockleshell ears
tucked close to her head, holding warmth
for when winter closes in, haystacks gathered
safely burrowed beneath the protection of snow.

Winters not cold enough to halt the march of beetles.
Snowpack not deep enough, so that pikas freeze
in their small scree tunnels. Some years too cold,
some years, a spring too late.

I'm on notebook number thirty-five,
some years had more to say, you see.

It's this unsteadying of the world
that has us all disassembling,
the human, the more-than-human,
all of us trying to put ourselves
and the pieces back into right place,
    no kintsugi master, no gold dust
      to beautify this weeping of trees.

## LAST CHRISTMAS
*by A.W. Glen*

In fall 2023, I do freelance proofreading of environmental research papers
I discover that the apocalypse is frequently short on commas
and I add them in
for $40 per 2500 words

Hours a day I comb for errors
absorb small details
dire warnings in dry language
countries failing to meet ~~NDCs~~<u>nationally determined contributions</u>
(Acronyms must be used more than 3x. Define acronyms in first use.)

I don't know science
just how to read
so I keep reading into things:
oil companies rebranding expensive <u>and inefficient</u> technologies
as climate mitigation tactics
getting them paid for by ~~government subsidies~~
<u>our future generations</u>
and profiting doubly

By the time dirty Winnipeg December
freakishly sops into view, bloated and feverish
sticky fluffless snow short on yuletide cheer
and the whole month groaning witchily about meeeelting,
I am convinced it's the Last Christmas
— and not in a Wham kind of way
(though the dread hits me almost onomatopoeically hard)

I imagine scientists raging and desperate
behind these bland white papers
marked boldly CONFIDENTIAL on the diagonal
Facts delivered emotionless, so their editor (me)
does not go into hysterics
print copies on the living room floor
(oblique-stamped secrecy be damned!)
run through downtown
distributing these deeply boring harbingers of doom
"Do you know what they're getting away with!"
Pages scattered soaking on the too warm too wet sidewalk
bleeding red Track Changes

My friends are tenderly annoyed at my prophesying
(I've been known to experience Anxiety)
We've of course agreed the world is ending
but the End might mean something different to them,
since they keep having babies

I miss the river trail
The Assiniboine gurgles unfrozen through the holidays
but I still need to buy gifts
and I'm grateful the demise I'm convinced of
is in want of a spell-check
($-wise, I'm doing quite well)

Half-hearted winter coughs a few times
gratefully forfeits into March
and smoky summer passes
December 2024 finds me reading poetry instead
a gentler job
heaviness shrouded in metaphor
removed of the urgency of jargon
I buy a real tree
and tentatively hope for a few more Christmases

## A DISTORTED PORTRAIT
*by Paul Akpomuje*

From the
Jungle I see you
come from. Do you
you have McDonald's?
Hahahaha…you don't?
Seems y'all in danger
and in poverty and
living in huts and
slums
right?
Yeah? Malaria
killing y'all in Africa, huh? No, I'm never going there, that mosquito-infested
continent. Do you have a history? Oh, I forgot, you were all slaves, shipped
to Europe & America as plantation
workers. You're one of the new
miserable migrants. Why are
you here? Where're you from?
When're you going back to…?
Shocking! So, you speak good
English? I expected you'd be
unintelligent. But…erm…you
talk somehow still. S-o-r-r-y,
what accent is that? It, erm
sounds funny & weird. Why
is there fighting in Africa?
I heard y'all are corrupt.

| Wonder | Why are |
| maybe | you all |
| it is a | loud & |
| lot of | lousy |
| corru | rude |
| ption | no-do |
| that | good- |
| leads | ers! & |
| to the | unruly |
| war in | baby- |
| Africa. | daddies |
| So unrefined | and…umm ba- |
| & primitive? | by mummies…? |

## BAD ACTORS
*by Adhika Ezra*

*When the post-pandemic boom cooled and businesses no longer needed the additional labour help, as a federal team, we could have acted quicker, and turned off the taps faster.*
—**Trudeau on immigration cuts**

We were warm water that rinsed your hands
Kept them clean and safe
Now we are sewage
Contaminating your illusions of security
Submissive to exploitation, we overcrowd housing, steal jobs
Flood the space

We are wastewater, the runoff
After *cheap foreign labour* has been wrung out of the body
After resource extraction, the tides swallow my home
Invisible hand plucks forests like flowers
After hungry men swallow cities as vitamins for growth

When you ask about my long-term plans, whether I will stay
I answer as if the decision is mine to make
As if the label *temporary* isn't tagged to my ear
As if how I look wasn't the reason you already knew to ask

*Sent home* is one way to say deported without uttering the word
I may be disposed of, but
After I drown, after you suffocate from insatiability
We flow out of the pipes and seep back into the same soil
To finally become borderless

# INVENTORY
*by Christina Shah*

part numbers murmured as
evening vespers by the paid faithful

warehouse calisthenics —
coworkers crouching to see
what sprockets lurk along lower shelves —
ancient cast-iron catfish
bottom-feeding

straining to reach overstock
abandoned haplessly
ten feet up

counting safety wands nested
into giant neon dildoes
while Dan is talking to himself in aisle B03

friday evening is far from over
and corporate has cast fried chicken
upon the waters

mice — migrants from the casino next door — drop in
and we sincerely hope the stateside auditor
does not spot them

*who fucked this up?* someone mutters
disturbing the dust
among a myriad of greased bearings
stainless steel lifesavers in a tube

an explosion of work gloves
with meathead superhero names
like *dogfight* and *stealth*

for saving yourself from yourself
when you slip
with the boxcutter

## HANGING LIGHTS AT THE ZOO
*by Cole Osiowy*

Standing at the tree
Feeling pretty good today
Working quietly
Wrote a poem

Thinking of Evan working at this tree
Yesterday
Standing here on this ladder
It's getting warmer out

Saw the squirrel monkey
And later waved hello
Also the thick-kneed bird
(Strange name, didn't match the picture)

## MAY I HELP YOU?
*by Myla Chartrand*

Mountains of plastic float in the ocean,
Mountains of plastic pile up in the back,
Gallons of oil spilled, wasted, ruined.
Clean-up on aisle three.

Mounting tensions as frontiers creep closer to the summit,
Mounting heat as ice turns to liquid gold.
Invade, drill, extract.
Restock the shelves.

Is any of this worth it?
Can I do anything from my $15.30/hr vantage point?
If I stop, someone else will step in to do it, and I'll be screwed.
The cogs do what they're told, and the machine wastes on.

Miss saying I never knew any of this.
Miss when winters didn't seem so warm.
Miss lying to myself about the exponential worsening of it all.
Miss when I didn't know how much trash there really is.

## THOSE DAYS BEFORE THE MINE

*(lyrics, to the tune of "Auld Lang Syne," in case the future needs a lament)*

by Jon Broderick

The rivers once were filled with reds
Ten million at a time.
Belugas and the brown bears fed
As salmon homeward climbed.

Fishermen, their families,
Their honest livings earned
When salmon from Pacific seas
To Bristol Bay returned.

> Those days before the mine, my friends
> Those days before the mine.
> Would we could have them back again,
> Those days before the mine.

'Twas nature free, untamed and wild
Far as the eye could see.
But here foul tailings now are piled
Until eternity.

At first "'Tis only trace," they said.
"Your fish will be just fine."
But leaching copper left them dead
That came from Pebble Mine.*

> Those days before the mine, my friends
> Those days before the mine.
> Would we could have them back again,
> Those days before the mine.

The water's clear and cold there yet
Aye, clear and cold and bare.
Now nothing lives in Nushagak
Though salmon once ran there.

---

* Pebble Mine is a proposed copper, gold, and molybdenum mine in the Nushagak and Kvichak river watersheds of Bristol Bay, Alaska.

# INTERVIEW AT SEA
*by Lindsay Bird*

Breakfast with the scientists and it's a lot
of eggs. Hungry after our shared

dawn, the ocean dead
calm, like it's way too early to get excited
about waves. A seal rises

into ripples.
I tell the ripples
I am recording, in keeping with the crystal
clearness of it all.

Scientists delighted their machine dove,
recorded pH and returned, dripping in robot
loyalty.

Like an underwater drone?
Exactly, you got it.

I don't really have anything.
Acidity carbon and water entangled
somehow, polyamorous.

How to explain this
to dry land. Wet notebook.

Wrong question. How does the crisis
make you feel?

The only grimace
of the morning, annoyed and yes at this point hungry.

Captain breaks up the silence with the bow
of his grandfather's boat, stories of the ice
surrounding that generation.

Stepping onto the wharf above
the halocline.

The haze where salt and freshwater meet.
Scientist giving me the name, a little gift.
What we do and do not
understand, underneath.

Did you get everything
you need? Close
enough. Let's go eat.

## TURTLES, WHERE CAN I SEE?
*by Mhao (em) Palevino*

*"Can you read this book for me?"*
Of course, I will ... *of course, I will.*

I love seeing your curious eyes sparkle,
As I read to you the story of the turtle named Yertle.
You ask me of his tale, his home,
What he eats, and where he roams.

As I read each line, all enthusiasm and cheer,
Your eyes grow big, lost in the story, unaware.
More than the message or how the story came to be,
You want to know *"turtles, where can I see?"*

My hands tremble, the pages feel thin,
A thought weighs on my chest, but I keep my grin.

Little ones, some turtles live in rivers, in sea,
Some eat mushrooms, berries, and sea jellies.
I have seen them before, in blue streams and reefs,
Yertle was not there — only the free.

Forgive me, there is another truth you should know,
The turtles, of land and sea, are losing their homes.
In danger of becoming just stories of tale and age,
Like Pterodactyls left on history's page.

There are also Yertles outside of the book,
They wear shells too, though not like the turtle's nook.
These Yertles are on two feet, destroying land and sea.
Scoff at every Mack. "Why care for turtles, you see?"

I am sorry to tell you
I know where some of the turtles would be.
In water, tangled in scraps, toxic oil on their skin
On land, left in dumps, threatened by Yertles' sins.

Though there remains the future that I fear,
I know your wonder will light the way, that much is clear
Keep searching for the turtles with all your might,
But when faced with the Yertles, stand up for what is right.

And so, I pray that when you are grown,
You will read this book differently than I have shown.
You will share the stories of turtles you have come to see,
And the Yertles you have fought to keep them free.

# A PRAYER FOR FISH
*by Hanako Teranishi*

My palms are pressed together
a moment of prayer for the fish and rice before me.
*Itadakimasu.*
*I humbly receive* the life
given in this meal, the life
I receive from the fish and the sea
and all that came before
and all that came after.

When I come into work, I enter from the back lane.
Past the garbage and past the bluefin tuna defrosting.
The smell of fish meat and bones warms my nose.

"High quality, it melts on your tongue"
is what I am told to say about hon maguro
to customers who are struggling to say *edamame*
or try to correct my tongue because they "were in Japan last summer,"
or the ones whose eyes gleam at the price.
It becomes a luxury to eat a dying population.

A group of men order the rest of the hon maguro for the table.
The pieces are balanced between flowers, upon shiso leaves and ice.
The platter freezes my fingers, I feel the condensation
from the bowl slowly pool in my palm, it weighs upon me
with every step. Their eyes sparkle when I place it on the table, and I imagine
they must be seeing pieces of pink gold. They drink and swear
and snap their fingers at me. Shoving glasses in my arms for more drinks.
I can see that the ice is melting and the bluefin starting to sink.

Maybe it's something about the "low-fi Japanese evening" playlist
that carries minds away. Or the lack caught in the soft dim lights
that makes it easy enough to forget. To forget. To forget a prayer.

At the end of the night, they leave licking sake and shoyu off their lips.
They leave behind the plate of unfinished bluefin and melting ice.
Four pieces left. *ichi, ni, san, shi.* An unlucky number, *shi* means *death.*
One piece falls through the ice and sinks to the bottom.

I become a lone pallbearer,
condensation pools in my palms and runs down my arms.
Meat and bones reunite in the garbage,
adorned with wilting flowers.

## ENTERING LANDSCAPE

*—after Melissa General*

*by Ellen Chang-Richardson*

————————————————————————water has conveyance———
a way of delivering its people its items its intangible infusions to form
the individual and our collective memory and somewhere in-between
the deep study of this connection to place to history and a soft desire
to hold on to gather to revitalize to recognize to understand and
to sift to sift to shift and to attempt to    reconcile this unresolved sense
of belonging of being of beginning and regaining   part of our ongoing
———strategy for survival—————————————————————

## A FARMER'S LAMENT
*by Leslie Kaup*

in April, briefly
water flowed in the creek
roared in the creek
washed clean two years
of drought
but now
a dry cracked trail
sunken in the woods
edged by willows singed and yellow
jack in the pulpit's bright fruits

when I was a landscaper
sometimes we built
dry stream beds
out of river rock
as a feature in a garden
this creek bed
where once water flowed
even beneath thick ice
now only
ghost of a creek
barren strip of cracked earth

## THERE HAS BEEN SOMETHING
*by Ed Edmo*

       sometimes it is a song
       sometimes a whisper
       sometimes it appears to be an animal
       then other times
       weeping
       I hear it

there has been something
that has disappeared
from my mother earth

I'm not sure what it was
but
       sometimes at night
       I can hear it in the wind
       or
              it comes to me
              in my dreams
              like
                      the smell of salmon
                          cooking

## WRITE THE RIVER
*by Lorri Neilsen Glenn*

She could burn the dream, at least it's fire,
something she will need when the cold sets in.
Lately, she shakes off tears, surely nothing

worse can happen. She aches for morning
light that once met her eyes, drew her down
to the path along the water where shore birds

knit the air with sound, deer bedded down
beyond her view and she could summon
words to honour them. Now she lingers

under blankets, wary of the day's signals,
zeros and ones and flashing lights, noise,
bloodshed, greed. Unknowing is impossible.

Are words — like a spring songbird or a shore
in a storm — in peril, skewed, their essence
muted? Meaning, usually a reliable span

across a chasm, ruptures, slips, becomes
treacherous. Her wily teacher — skinwalker,
*wisakedjak* — calls her now to look. Like

the rare deer on the field at dusk: slow
down. Listen. Sniff the air. Be alert. In chaos
and calamity, words, like any tool, must be

held steady, find their bearings in silence,
away from the madding rabble. Like a river,
words know their time. There is no hurry.

## ANTHOLOGIST'S HAIKU
*by Melanie Dennis Unrau*

swap anthology
for jury duty still tuned
to courtroom, landfill

at workshops poets
count hurricane syllables
tell wildfire stories

poster is ready
tires crack november puddles
last bike ride this year

cold snap no poems
sidewalk staple gun sun dogs
no soliciting

an editor's friends:
candles incense wicked groans
of windowsill plants

walk to the river
look for living things: a fox!
(she moves under ice)

a boycott a book
launch your lyrics make me weep
i'm not all frozen

another climate
meeting missed instead shovel
spring melt work poems

forward foreword hum
breakup songs for my career
my friend the river

## UNDEFEATED: A ROOFER'S HAIKU
*by Gabriel "ArchAngel" Ehijie*

The roof leaks in rain,
The house is flooded with tears,
Yet my walls still stand.

# GOOD INDIAN
*by Caleigh Miller*

Storm of a century, it was
Or at least the worst I'd seen in all my years, all 20 of them.
Begging, pleading with them
Can we do this interview another way
Another time?
The job doesn't start for 3 more months.
Everyone says not to go — it's not safe
I need a job. This job.
It could lead to a career, if I do everything just right.
It's too cold, I can't see the road
We need to see if you are good enough
We're looking for a good Indian. I mean, Aboriginal.
That's what they call you now, isn't it?

I drove for 8 hours. Snow swirling, Prairie wind screaming
Yellowhead's blacktop, black ice.
White knuckles.
It's too cold, I can't see the road
Finally made it. Road weary and ragged.
On time.

Smoothing invisible wrinkles from my borrowed blazer. Good enough.
Empty boardroom, white walls
Speaker phone crackles
It was too dangerous for them to drive, they said.
But thank God an Indian finally showed up.
I mean, Aboriginal. That's what they call you now, isn't it?
Can you come back again, later?
When it's safe for us to drive.

Weeks later, storm has passed. In the past.
Can you come back? We are still looking for someone.
Should I?
I risked my life for this once. I can't go back.

Okay, they said. It's okay.
I guess we can hire you anyway.
You'll be good enough.

## STEAMED VIVIANE
*by Keith Inman*

She filled the Steam Jenny with water,
yanked it to her assigned area,
turned on the steam and blasted away at parts
strewn across the factory floor
when a bolt clacked her face shield.
Georg neighed from across the aisle,
"Fuck off Short Shift. You're getting us wet."
She unhitched her burro and led
its shiny steel ass to the next section
where the sprayer barely pissed anything.
Off came the helmet, face shield and hoodie
of her yellow-rubber bubble suit.
She decided to have coffee.

At the window, she counted rats
playing in a foam slick along the ravine
running red to the river
as a breeze dried the sweat of her brow.

She spied Simon sidling up the aisle.
"You done here?" he asked.
She kicked at the machine's stainless belly,
"This thing's shitless."
Simon smirked, "How far'd ya get?"
"First section."
"For Chrissake."
"*You* figure this stupid-ass mule out!"
Georg swept by, "Steam's back on."
"How long's it been off for?"
"Hour or so," he smiled, and strolled away
with a wrench weighing the arse of his pants.
"Get the machine clean," Simon brayed.
She nodded toward a flood of dark oil pooling a drain.
"Not Your Concern," Simon said,
and pointed at the machine.
She fingered the trigger and a powerful stream
scoured a wild *G* across the floor.
She finished the sentence, *eorg is an ass!*

## BROOKLYN-QUEENS TORNADOES
### September 16, 2010
*by Davidson Garrett*

Driving my taxi during Manhattan's
evening twilight, a blue-suited male
hails me, requesting a ride to Maspeth —
a terrible fare to begin my night shift.

Customer plops his ass in backseat
with me behind the steering wheel
as grey clouds burst from a dark sky
pouring heavy rain — soaking cab tires

rolling to the antiquated Ed Koch Bridge.
Luckily, we are safe, as sharp hail pounds
the metal roof. Over the iron behemoth
into Queens, traffic grinds to a dead halt —

taillights blink through wet windshield.
I stop my wipers as fierce storm ends
while glued to dashboard radio news —
reporting twisters hit Queens & Brooklyn

toppling massive trees & power lines
covering city streets — blocking roadways.
All subways completely shut down
serving areas foreign to whirling vortexes.

Peering in my rearview mirror, I mutter —
"I'm turning off the meter cause we're stuck."
The passenger's commute usually a breeze
but my yellow canary becomes a tortoise

trailing thousands of honking motorists.
I introduce myself to my lone hostage
who quips, "I'm Phil, an exhausted banker."
Trapped together, bemoaning our fate —

I maneuver wheels past broken branches
following buses and box trucks — baffled
tornadoes struck Gotham instead of Kansas.
Swerving on backstreets — weaving in jams

gridlock worse — streetlights blown out
inching in pitch black without progress.
The taxi's high beams guide us —
a futile effort with angry automobiles

ahead — confused off this beaten path
moving block by block, slow as molasses.
Phil & I begin to seriously bullshit —
after two hours, he snoozes with naps.

Awaking again, we continue disclosing
life stories to each other — strangers
hashing over what destined our opposite
career paths. We divulge deepest secrets

confessing intimately — difficult trials
& heartbreaks we've both endured.
Finally, eerie midnight — arriving
before a classic Archie Bunker house

we finish our surreal odyssey
replete with much taxicab therapy.
I tell Phil, "This hellish trip's on me" —
but he hands me a wad of green cash.

# APPENDIX A
*by Ruchini Abayakoon*

when i say i live on belly rubs i mean
the pitter patter of firefly wings bumping
against the inside of my stomach
every time i feel the loom of a deadline
pour rain on my head before i ever
manage to pull out an umbrella or at least
              a cap                   i mean the ceaseless tap dance from
                                    a thousand centipedes fighting for my
                              attention as i scroll through for hours and
                                  stop for less than a second on each,
                        zealously holding so tight to myself that i
                          have refused to give my mind or body
                                to anything too fully so no,
                    i no longer own myself in any capacity,
                                        either —

i mean the bubbling that starts at the
pit of my stomach and bubbles up to
my throat like bile every time i talk to you
and listen to your life of binaries. where
the self care bubble refuses to coexist
with any other form of care
where caring about two things at once
is a radical notion that you are comfortably
              distanced from.           i live on belly rubs the way monarchs
                          live on the poison that the milkweed created
                                    to ward them off.
                          the way my heart beats incessantly
                      even when i will it to stop for a moment
                                  to have a breather.
              it knows not to rest, and it leads by example so i follow it
                        every day as it falls to my stomach for
                          a temporary stop and i feel it
                    against my palm when i look for a swollen
                                    appendix —

# SACRIFICE
*by Sydney Taylor*

what is labour?
is it the harsh metal, wood planks, beaten nails
and time we'll never get back?
maybe it's sitting in an office 8 hours a day,
watching the sun rise and fall from within grey walls.
is it a CEO making big deals above our heads,
trading our lives like
playing cards?
what is labour when we are too sick to work?
where do we fall
when no amount of worker's rights will protect us from starving,
from choking on
black smoke when we open our windows in the summer?
i feel the effects of our crumbling world
in my body.
watch out my window
as sickness rises like the current,
washing across my city.
i reach out from across my screen,
watching hospital workers flee,
leaving the sick to their fate of hurricane winds.
my breathing becomes laboured.
*only the things you can control*
but what can I control
when you sacrifice my life to grease the wheels of the machine?
how do I fight when I have so little left to give?
when warming weather leaves me holed up in bed for weeks,
hands swelling in the constricting heat.
how many of my dreams do I have to let go?
my wheelchair won't work in the water.
*deep breaths*
*let this radicalize you rather than lead you to despair,*
i repeat in front of the mirror
an endless refrain easing my collapse,
*there's work to be done.*

# THE SWARMING HIVE
*by Carla Harris*

our office is built for
division, mixing spit with fibres of weathered
wood we gnaw, retch and assemble
the comb, marking our well-earned
cubicles with kitschy gifts and artless pages
stamped with crests, laced
with chancellors' signatures
for proving we deserve
approval

the spring teems with coming queens
who fiercely build a future city, a fertile
army of carriers, the yellowjackets chew
last year's growth to retch up walls
with our spit, until

the heat of aspiration invades
'til one succumbs, and the company turns
faintly as a pot of tea, growing slowly
golden as authority
racing to out-build each other through the night
our eyes flitting and piercing in the lurking
threshold of budding rivalry

as there is only ever one *true* queen

the boss's assistant is bringing coffees for *her regulars*
eight of us drink coffee every morning but *her regulars*
add up to seven, so I walk to the Tim's, and recall the humming
mornings back when we'd wait
                         together, fluid as family

until the world we built demonstrates
            as we sway,     dangling
      from the dying branch

walking through the dark cafeteria
a black wall of windows poses as mirrors
I'm shocked to see my empty hands are fists
        my shoulders rise to boil
                on growing steam, the screaming
                        kettle on the stove

## DOING RECONCILIATION WORK IN WÎNIPÊK
*by Jamie Paris*

Is writing about reconciliation
integral to the work of forgiveness?
Does teaching students about
reconciliation help to create
a more just prairie city?
Maybe. But writing and teaching are not enough
for Wînipêk to become a kinder, gentler
and more just place; we have to do the work
to dance positive peace into being.
We're doing the labour of cultivating
Change.

Reconciliation is physically, emotionally,
and psychologically exhausting.
Learning the truth about colonial violence
in Indian Residential Schools in Canada is
distressing. Teaching our history honestly is
Uncomfortable.

Have you heard about the time people planted two hundred
tiny wood craft crosses with orange bows
under the pedestal of a toppled queen?
Such difficult, careful, emotional work.
Each one represented a kidnapped child
who should have grown up at home, and
who ought to have been sent home to their parents
after their breath was unjustly taken.
Beside this loving work of public protest
men slept in a teepee, in November,
keeping a sacred fire, to light a way home
for the children and their brave and bereaved
Families.

My labour towards reconciliation
began with an uneasy realization
that all the kidnapped and abused children,
every single one of them, is my kin.

Every missing mother, sister, aunty,
and cousin. Every single one of them
is my kin, and I have to help them come
Home.

I know what it means to grow up
with a mother-sized hole at the dinner table.
Reconciliation would be knowing that
our losses are temporary, that the missing
will return to us spiritually unharmed.
Reconciliation work happens because
we know it takes an engaged village
to put up flyers, organize good searches
and lobby racist police to serve
to honour their commitments.
Imagine all the joyful work we could do,
if we created a just little city
where the work of reconciliation became
Unnecessary.

Reconciliation work is dragging the Red
slowly and carefully, looking for stolen
sisters after the police refuse
to search for our missing relatives.
Reconciliation would look like searching the landfill
for the bodies of murdered women and
girls, because families deserve closure
without having to go on television
and beg the provincial government for
Justice.

Reconciliation work looks like a clan
of bears walking on North End streets at night
handing out naloxone and blankets.
Reconciliation work tries to re-build
community while preventing the next
Catastrophe.

The work is impossibly difficult
but it might be easier if we do it
Together.

## ABOVE EPILIMNION, WARMING TOO
*by Tazi Rodrigues*

we went fishing for minnows but
pulled up heat instead, flashed metal mesh
against the sun. five empty traps on a

string. earlier this summer, we excavated
the shoreline for stones to sink
sampling equipment to the cold

bottom of the lake. fished
trout out of weak hypolimnion before
it settled thick into layers, before

stratification stuck to the sand.
after early may flooded, we only had
a few days for fish surgeries,

pressed between the netted hours of spring
monitoring. white sucker white sucker pearl
dace white sucker & finescale & finescale.

fish on the measuring board, us
in our cardboard-brown rain
suits. at breakfasts, the lake trout

students (me & v) lamented the thermometers,
how fast the water was warming though
the ice peeled off so far into the

year — though last summer we passed
each other in smoke, waterbomber belly almost
skimming the shore. later, i'll find these years

back to back in a list of extremities. i'll be watching
v's drone footage of trout foraging at subaqueous
cliffs from my cubicle, laced with my deskmate's newly

invaded invertebrates. now i pivot the boat to
cold shoulder by Fish Rock, only place of this whole
lake with shade — this scorched afternoon. m pours

water overboard from our buckets & i let water
out of the boat. we drink litres of it,
collect ourselves from the waves. this may

be what it feels like to tread water and it might
be what it feels like before we sink.

# EMOTIONAL LABOUR
*by Eesha Nilan*

Oysters are the filter feeders of the ocean: underwater empaths who take it all in, rhythmically composting plankton and parasite, sediment and sorrow. Highly sensitive types, attuned to the needs of the saline collective, circulating nutrients and soothing echoes of whalesong. This work of co-regulating the marine nervous system relies on porous membranes, a trait common to bivalve molluscs and workers in helping professions. People forget that pearls are made from grief — jewelled evidence of wounds sustained while siphoning toxins from the turbid torrent of capitalism. In the mantle between our soft bodies and hinged shells, we offer surrogacy to this hurt. A gestational healing occurs, milky minerals blurring the boundary between "self" and "other." What estuaries and neuroscientists know is that resilience is relational. That is to say, it is cultivated among us not within us. A pro-social response to the effluent of an economy that externalizes the cost of caring. It's no wonder they call it compassion fatigue. For once our sweet mollusc meat is extracted, we lay discarded and calcified in sun-bleached heaps. Like tidal crones, retired from lifelong labour, our iridescent wombs still refracting the world's salty gaze.

## THE CONTRIBUTORS

**Levy Abad** writes for *Pilipino Express* in Winnipeg. He has two published books about Filipino activists and musicians in Winnipeg, *Giving Back, Paying Forward* and *Rhythms and Resistance*. He was a member of a workers' cultural group of the May 1st labour movement (KMU) in the Philippines. Currently, he works as a baker/oven and stacker operator.

**Ruchini Abayakoon** is a PhD candidate in the environmental humanities, exploring the intersection of postcolonial studies, environmental justice, and Sri Lankan literature. She is also an earring maker, writer, emerging plant mom, and avid people-watcher.

**Peace Akintade-Oluwagbeye,** Saskatchewan Poet Laureate, is an African-Canadian interdisciplinary poet and chorus-poem playwright residing in Saskatoon, Saskatchewan. Organically from Yorubaland Nigeria, Peace explores the intersectionality of the artist community by dipping her honey-stained fingers into poetry, dance, performance art, critical research, and the theatre world. Peace is a recipient of the RBC SaskArts Emerging Artist Award and the Platinum Jubilee Queen's Medal.

**Paul Akpomuje** is a doctoral candidate at Queen's University. His work explores visa stories, poetics of migration, identity, black studies, and social justice. He co-convened The Poetics of Migration, an event that intersects poetry with community stories to unpack issues of displacement and belonging, immigration paperwork, and the onerous work of travelling while black.

**Hari Alluri** is author of *Tabako on the Windowsill* (Brick Books, 2025), *The Flayed City* (Kaya, 2017), and chapbook *Our Echo of Sudden Mercy* (Next Page, 2022). A migrant poet, editor, and facilitator whose work includes dock crew, warehouse, construction, landscaper, and bookseller, his award-winning writing is published widely.

**Anjali Appadurai** is Director of Campaigns with the Climate Emergency Unit and the Director of the Padma Centre for Climate Justice. The Padma Centre is a hub for diasporic communities across Canada to build power around issues of climate and economic justice. Anjali has worked as a climate activist and campaigner for over fifteen years.

**Kurt Armstrong** is a builder, writer, and lay Anglican minister. He lives in the West Broadway neighbourhood of Winnipeg with his family.

**Mike Bagamery** lives in Winnipeg, Manitoba, on Treaty One territory. He is neurodivergent/"disabled." He has served as an organizer for the Canadian Council on Invasive Species, as a parliamentary intern through GreenPAC, and as a fundraiser for the Wilderness Committee. He provides holistic research for mass movements.

**Ikeoluwapo B. Baruwa** is a PhD candidate in the Faculty of Education at Queen's University, Canada. He has served as an occupational health and safety officer at PSAC 901, Queen's University. Currently, he is a certified joint health and safety committee co-chair and a steward in the Faculty of Education.

**Jessica Bebenek** (she/her) is a queer, chronically ill poet & interdisciplinary artist who has earned her living as a cashier, a waitress, an independent publisher, a childcare provider, a teaching assistant, a textile artist, a risograph printer, a bookmaker, a community workshop leader, a professor, and, somehow, a poet. Find Jessica online at www.jessicabebenek.art / @notyrmuse.

**Dr. Renée E. Mazinegiizhigoo-kwe Bédard** is Anishinaabeg, Kanien'kehá:ka, and French Canadian. She is a member of Dokis First Nation, Ontario, Canada. Currently, she is an Assistant Professor at Western University in both the Gender, Sexuality, and Women's Studies Department and the Indigenous Studies program. Her research primarily focuses on Anishinaabeg women, motherhood, traditional knowledge, and maternal culture.

**Ross Belot** is a poet, photographer, translator, filmmaker, and op-ed writer on climate change inaction. Before all that, he worked for over three decades in the fossil-fuel industry. His latest poetry collection is *Moving to Climate Change Hours* (Wolsak & Wynn, 2020). He lives in Hamilton, Ontario sometimes.

**Lindsay Bird** is a poet and documentary maker. As a journalist, she's interested in covering contemporary realities of rural Canada, as well as climate change. Her first poetry collection, *Boom Time* (Gaspereau, 2019), is a semi-autobiographical collection set in the oil sands of Fort McMurray.

**Jon Broderick** has been a commercial salmon fisherman since 1976, first as a deckhand seining in Kodiak, then gillnetting in Southeast Alaska and, since 1988, running the family set net outfit each summer in Bristol Bay, Alaska. He, his wife Doreen, and most of his family live off-season on the Oregon coast.

**David C. Brydges** is a Construction & General Workers Union Local 92 member in Edmonton, Alberta. He is artistic director of Spring Pulse Poetry Festival in Northern Ontario and "Poet Emissary" for the Ontario Poetry Society. David published two chapbooks about the oil sands, *Anthologies of the Misshapen* and *Crude Truths*.

**Jane Byers** has published two memoirs, *Coming Home from the Candy Factory* (2025) and *Small Courage* (2020), and two poetry collections, *Acquired*

*Community* (2016) and *Steeling Effects* (2014), with Caitlin Press. She was the 2018 Writer in Residence for SFU's Archives of Lesbian Oral Testimony and is an ergonomist. She has poems and essays published in anthologies and literary journals including *Best Canadian Poetry 2014*. Find more on her website: janebyerswriter.com.

**Ellen Chang-Richardson** is an award-winning poet, multi-genre writer, judicial assistant, and co-founder of Riverbed Reading Series. The author of *Blood Belies* (Wolsak & Wynn, 2024), their work has appeared in *Augur*, *Grain*, *Plenitude*, *Room*, *Watch Your Head*, and more. They write to shine a light. Find out more at www.ehjchang.com.

**Myla Chartrand** is a writer, storyteller, and an avid lover of words of all kinds. Her previous job as a minimum-wage retail employee now shapes both her creative endeavours as well as her approach to the global climate crisis.

**Rina Garcia Chua** (she/her/siya) is a creative and critical scholar from the Philippines, with publications in magazines and journals worldwide. She has been a migrant mother, an advocate for migrant rights, a university instructor and administrator, and an ecopoet. Rina is the author of the poetry collection *A Geography of (Un)Natural Hazards* (Sampaguita, 2025).

**Jean Clipsham** is a retired public health nurse/nurse practitioner. Her poem is about how climate-change action has become the focus of her life in retirement and about ageism, which exists even in the climate-change movement.

**Fiona Conway** worked on Canada's national suicide crisis line (now 988) between 2021 and 2023, where she often encountered the despair very young people felt about their future in a rapidly warming world. Fiona is now studying medicine, hoping to work with children, and keeping their fear in mind.

**Renee Cronley** is a writer from Manitoba who stepped away from nursing to prioritize her children and has been channeling her knowledge and experiences into a poetry book about nursing burnout. Renee can be found at www.reneecronley.com.

**Jim Daniels** is from a family of Detroit autoworkers. His grandfather worked for Packard, his father worked for Ford's, his brother worked for Chrysler's. Jim also worked at Ford's — it paid for college. A retired educator, Jim now tries to honour this history, and these lives, in his writing.

**Jennifer deGroot** lives and works with her family on Big Oak Farm near Morden, Manitoba. Her days are filled with raising kids, making food, gardening, cheesemaking, beekeeping, tending chickens and sheep, natural dyeing, sewing, knitting, friends, reading, walking, teaching English to new Canadians, and a whole lot of dishwashing.

**Justene Dion-Glowa** is a queer Métis internationally published author, artist, and death doula. Their award-nominated debut collection, *Trailer Park Shakes* (Brick), was released in 2022. They have been diligently working within the non-profit industrial complex for 13 years, hoping that someday something they do will change someone's life for the better.

**Amanda Donnelly** lives in Winnipeg, Manitoba, on Treaty One territory, where she works as a massage therapist. She is a mother, wife, coffee-lover, and retro video game enthusiast.

**Martin Durkin** is a Canadian writer with three published books; he also works in security. His stories have appeared in *The Bay Today* from North Bay, Ontario. In 2024 several poems and stories were published in the anthology *Otherwise Engaged*, vol 14. Security has been part of Durkin's ongoing narrative.

**Trisia Eddy Woods** (she/her) is the author of *A Road Map for Finding Wild Horses* (Turnstone, 2024). A former editor for Red Nettle Press, Trisia's writing has appeared in a variety of literary journals and chapbooks across North America. She and her family, both human and nonhuman, reside in Treaty 6 territory.

**Ed Edmo** is a Shoshone-Bannock poet, playwright, storyteller, tour guide, and lecturer/consultant on Northwest tribal culture. He grew up in Celilo Falls on the Columbia River. The river was a welcome playmate that never had been called in for dinner. He watched the falls being flooded March 10, 1957. He has the thunder of the falls in his heart.

**Gabriel "ArchAngel" Ehijie** is a Canadian based Nigerian spoken-word poet, screenwriter, and aspiring filmmaker. The 2021 winner of the Institute of Afrikology Resource Centre's "Heritage Month Poetry Competition" and co-author of the book *Isles* (Soyos, 2022) is an alumnus of the University of Regina, with a season's experience in residential roofing.

**Kristian Enright** is a Treaty One writer who will be publishing a full-length book of poetry called *Postmodern Weather Report* (Turnstone, 2025) that deals with climate change. He is also working on several other projects, including a long poem and a collection of short stories called "The Book of Conversations."

**Adhika Ezra** is an Indonesian social studies graduate student and organizer. His hope is sustained by the communities that surround him — communities made of people who embody care and refuse to be apathetic in a society that normalizes violence.

**Sanita Fejzić** is a poet, playwright, and writer who grows tomatoes, strawberries, peppers, lettuce, beans, cucumbers, radishes, and other edibles. The child of Bosniak peasants, Sanita is the first in her family born in the city. She lives on the unceded territory of the Algonquin Anishinaabeg people in Ottawa.

**Brad Fougere** is an IWW member working to build an independent shopfloor committee at his workplace on unceded unsurrendered Mi'kmaq territory. He plays bass in post-metal band Burdened and is more hopeful than his poem might suggest.

**Alex Gallo-Brown** is a labour organizer and writer who lives in Seattle. He is the author of *Variations of Labor* (Chin Music, 2019), a collection of poems and short stories, and *The Language of Grief* (2012), a collection of poems.

**Davidson Garrett** is a poet and actor living in New York City. He drove a yellow taxi for 40 years to supplement his artistic pursuits. Davidson is the author of two poetry collections and is a member of the Worker Writers School led by the poet Mark Nowak.

**A.W. Glen** is a Winnipeg-based musician, writer, and editor. She recently published her first novel, *Bukowski's Broken Family Band* (2024), on Transistor 66 Records. She once worked herself into a panic doing freelance editing for environmental NGOs, but she's currently enjoying gentler work as the managing editor for *Contemporary Verse 2*.

**Claire Gordon**'s (she/her) ecofeminist interest was first sparked while working in provincial parks assessing hazard trees, clearing and bucking windfall, maintaining trails, and building boardwalks. Recently, she's been participating in slope and stream channel stabilization with Redd Fish Restoration. Claire is a writer and photographer (35mm) based in Yuułuʔiłʔatḥ (Ucluelet, BC).

**Kanin Gosbee** is both a father and an artist, therefore it is his job to reflect the world we live in. Through his own experiences as well as others that inspire him, he breaks down concepts and reforms them into something that is more digestible for an audience.

**Lance Guilbault** is Cree and Anishinaabe from Fisher River Cree Nation and Roseau River Anishinaabe Nation. He believes that sobriety is life. Writing and teaching are passions for Lance, trying to inspire his students to walk upon Mother Earth mino-pimatisiwin, in a good way. Tobacco down, prayers up.

**Yolanda Hansen** lives and writes on Treaty 4 where she works with the Saskatchewan Writers' Guild and is a mom to two energetic boys. Her work has appeared in *Briarpatch, Deep Wild Journal,* and *Mantis* and is supported by SK Arts. She lives in Regina with her family.

**Carla Harris** (they/she) is a neurodivergent disabled, queer enby writer, performer, and interdisciplinary artist from Treaty 4 territory, living in Regina, Saskatchewan. They have had publications with the League of Canadian Poets, *Antilang*, and Frog Hollow Press. Harris teaches creative improvisation and is constantly writing in unconfined #CripTime.

**Alison Holliday** is a Scottish Immigrant living on Treaty One Land in Winnipeg, Manitoba. She graduated from the University of Manitoba in 2023 and has been working part-time jobs in theatre production and retail since. Her day-to-day labour consists of selling things, database mass reduction, and waiting for the phone to ring.

**Olivia Ingram** has mostly worked as a barista in non-unionized cafes in so-called Vancouver. Their art examines how urban spaces and subjects are shaped by moments, class, and geophysical capitalism. Olivia's poetry has been published in independent magazines and an experimental-writing anthology. They hold a couple of English degrees from Canadian universities.

**Keith Inman** worked as a steamfitter and troubleshooter (troublemaker) in the paper industry. Now, over fifty libraries worldwide carry his books. Some of Keith's favourite pastimes are canoeing, gardening, and maintaining his old limestone home, with his wife, in Niagara. The Indo-European language says his name means "of the forest."

**James Croal Jackson** is a Filipino-American poet working in film production. His latest chapbook is *A God You Believed In* (Pinhole, 2023). Recent poems are in *Iterant, Skipjack Review,* and *The Indianapolis Review.* He edits *The Mantle Poetry* from Nashville, Tennessee. Find more information at jamescroaljackson.com.

**SJ Jones** is a mixed-race African Nova Scotian and white settler. They are currently a PhD student in the History Department at Dalhousie University where they are researching the significant agricultural contributions made by the enslaved and free Black population in 18th-century Mi'kma'ki. They tend a flock of 12 Icelandic sheep.

**Leslie Kaup** lives in southern Minnesota with her husband, Bill, and various critters. She is a cook, farmer, activist, antiques dealer, and writer.

**Karen Loucks** (formerly Chester) lives on Vancouver Island, BC, the unceded traditional territory of the lək̓ʷəŋən speaking peoples. She worked as a park naturalist for many years. Her poetry has been published in several anthologies, was longlisted for the CBC Poetry Prize (2023), and won the High Marsh Press chapbook contest (2024).

Past Tofino Poet Laureate **Christine Lowther** has published four poetry collections and edited two poetry anthologies. Her memoir *Blockade: Diaries of a Forest Defender* was published in 2025 by Caitlin Press. Her two day jobs are Assistant at Vancouver Island Regional Library in Tofino's Legion basement, and cleaning at Tofino General Hospital.

**Rob Madden** is a writer and labourer living on the traditional and unceded territories of the Squamish and Tsleil-Waututh nations in the City of North Vancouver, BC. "I Strap the Suit On" was inspired by sand-blasting work. He is currently employed by Canada Post.

**Lia M. Markin** is a Colombian-Jewish poet and writer whose work explores identity, trauma, and migration. Drawing from years of experience in call centres, healthcare, and working with marginalized communities, her writing delves into themes of survival, displacement, and systemic inequities.

**M.S. Marquart** (she/her) is a disabled, mixed race Asian American emerging poet. Her writing seeks to shed light on the hidden daily lives of people living with long COVID and myalgic encephalomyelitis/chronic fatigue syndrome (ME/CFS). You can find her on Instagram at @m_s_marquart or at www.msmarquart.com.

**Caitlin McCullam-Arnal** (she/her) is a paid Data Collections Clerk and substitute teacher. For free, she loves her six cats, two dogs, and a partner who is a farmer/rancher. She worked for an oilfield service company in Treaty 4, southwest Saskatchewan, where she now lives. Her work-in-progress includes a novel and a poetry manuscript about cougars.

**Leah McInnis** is an artist and researcher from Fort McMurray, AB. She has worked as an arts administrator, educator, designer, technician, consultant, and assistant in cities throughout Canada to support her studio practice. Leah is currently working on an Interdisciplinary PhD in Media & Artistic Research at the University of Regina.

**Duncan Mercredi** is a Cree-mixed (Métis) writer/storyteller born in Misipawistik aka Grand Rapids, MB and now lives in Winnipeg, MB. His poem "blue collar memories" covers his blue collar days working with MB Highways and Manitoba Hydro.

**Caleigh Miller** (she/her) is a Métis woman from Saskatchewan who now calls the Yukon home. She works in Human Resources, advocating for diversity, equity, accessibility, and inclusion, and consideration of a Northern and Indigenous lens to make work better for people.

**Lisa Mulrooney** is a teacher in Stony Plain, Alberta. For 12 years, her husband worked rotational shift work at remote oil sands sites near Fort McKay. A former Poet Laureate of Stony Plain, Lisa co-founded Parkland Poets' Society and holds a master's in creative writing from Teesside University, UK.

**Lorri Neilsen Glenn,** author and contributing editor of fifteen titles of poetry, nonfiction and scholarly work, was Halifax's first Métis Poet Laureate. Professor Emerita at Mount Saint Vincent University and a University of King's College MFA mentor, her latest book is *The Old Moon in Her Arms: Women I Have Known and Been* (Nimbus, 2024).

**Eesha Nilan** is a neuroqueer writer in their forties who turned to poetry while on a career sabbatical due to disability. Their work weaves themes of hybridity, queer ecology, and coming into age as a second-generation South Asian immigrant and interdisciplinary educator living in K'emk'emeláy̓ (Vancouver).

**Cole Osiowy** is a young man, born and raised in Winnipeg. In 2023 he dropped out of art school to hang Christmas lights for a living.

**Ray Owen** is a seasonal labourer and aspiring writer who moves around Western Canada. He is passionate about the environment and the modern application of mythology.

**Lena Palacios** is a queer, disabled, mixed-race Chicana with Tepehuana and settler ancestry. They play with their cats/muses, Sonny, Sher, and Kimchi, when not writing on the run. She won the 2024 Quebec Writers' Federation's carte blanche prize and was shortlisted for *The Fiddlehead*'s 2024 Creative Nonfiction Contest and *The Malahat Review*'s 2025 Open Season Awards (Poetry).

**Mhao (em) Palevino** is a 29-year-old immigrant from the Philippines. Most of her past work aimed at serving marginalized sectors and the environment. Now here in Canada, she does her best to still be an advocate for others through her new path in early childhood education.

**Catherine Parceaud** is an English as a Second Language college teacher at a francophone Cégep in Rimouski, Quebec. She has also taught French and English primary school in Nunavik, Northern Quebec.

**Judy Parceaud** was born near London, England in 1940. She moved to Windsor in 1947 with her family where she grew up cherishing nature and open spaces. In 1963 she moved to Canada as a young bride, settling in Northern Quebec. Thrifty and frugal values have guided her throughout her life.

**Marjorie Poor** is an editor for a provincial government. She is also the editor of *Prairie books NOW* and a fiction editor at *Prairie Fire*. Her poems have appeared in *Vallum*, *CV2*, and *Prairie Fire*, and her chapbook of centos, *Voices [That] Haunt Us*, was published by JackPine Press in 2024.

**Ashley Qilavaq-Savard** is an Inuk poet, writer, artist, and filmmaker born and raised in Iqaluit, Nunavut. Her first book of poetry, *Where the Sea Kuniks the Land* (Inhabit, 2023), explores themes of decolonization, intergenerational trauma, language, and love for Inuit Nunangat.

**Bonnie Quan Symons** has had her poems published in journals in Canada, the United States, and Australia. She worked for Canadian universities and hospitals as a secretary/program assistant. She currently works at BC Teachers' Federation in Vancouver, Canada. She belongs to Pandora's Collective, Poetic Justice, and Writers' International Network (WIN) Canada.

**Tazi Rodrigues** (she/her) is a writer, aquatic biologist, and data wrangler for her neighbourhood pollinator garden. From Winnipeg, she currently lives on the unceded land of the Anishinaabe Algonquin Nation (Ottawa, ON). Her poems have recently appeared in *Arc Poetry Magazine*, *CV2*, and *The Malahat Review*.

**Ron Romanowski** is from North End Winnipeg. He was a postal worker, shop steward, and union activist. Injured on the job, his CUPW contract allowed him to retire, using his writing to remain active in progressive politics. Ron's tenth book of poetry, *10,000 Dancers Working Off Broadway*, was published by Augustine Hand Press in spring 2025.

**Ivan A. Salazar M.**, a passionate poet from a rich literary tradition, captures the human condition in his work. As the author of three bilingual poetry collections, *Temporal Echoes* (2024), *Weaver of Dreams* (2025), and *If You Head South* (2025), he bridges cultures through his words.

**Christina Shah** works in heavy industrial sales in Vancouver. Her poetry has appeared in numerous journals, was shortlisted for 2021's Ralph Gustafson Prize, and was selected for *Best Canadian Poetry 2023*. *rig veda* (Anstruther) was released in 2023; *if: prey, then: huntress* (Nightwood) in fall 2025.

**Kate Siklosi** is a poet, publisher, scholar, and third-generation oil and gas worker in the Chemical Valley of Sarnia, Ontario for a few summers where she worked as a labourer in several petrochemical plants. Her current work is in employment equity, and her creative work includes *Selvage* (Invisible, 2023) and *leavings* (Timglaset, 2021). She is co-founding editor of Gap Riot Press.

**Credell Simeon** is a Black Canadian who was born and raised in Grenada, where she visits often. She currently lives and works in Saskatchewan. She is a passionate writer, storyteller, and published researcher in data science. Her powerful storytelling brings light to the need for communities to build climate resiliency and sustainability.

**Sabrina Spenser Smith** is a former roofer from Regina who currently works as a copywriter in Winnipeg. In 2023, she published her first poetry collection, *A Brief Relief from Hunger* (Gordon Hill), which explores the toxic drug crisis in British Columbia.

**Jessica Smithies** is a queer writer currently living in Winnipeg, Manitoba. She currently works full time for an insurance brokerage. Her piece "Fire Season" reflects her experience working in a call centre during the 2023 Kelowna fire. In her free time, Jessica enjoys writing, reading, and playing with cats.

Nearly 30 years ago, **Ella Soper** worked in BC, planting black spruce seedlings and cottonwood poplar whips, climbing high into the branches of mature evergreens and pruning her way down, and burning slash. She now lives in

Ontario and has a daughter who works in the Interior as an Archeological Field Technician.

**Dani Spinosa** has too many jobs and not enough job security. She works as an adjunct professor, a software developer, a publisher and founding co-editor at the feminist micropress Gap Riot, managing editor of the *Electronic Literature Directory*, President at the feminist literary journal *Canthius*, and an amateur gardener.

**Sydney Taylor** is a spoken word poet and multidisciplinary artist from Treaty 4 territory. They have done paid and unpaid work in environmental activism and disability justice. Disabled organizers often perform uncompensated and unrecognized labour for our communities, and Sydney's poem is a nod to the work they do while barely staying afloat themselves.

**Luana Terán** is a queer woman from Barranquilla, Colombia. She moved to Canada in 2023 and is studying creative writing in college. She previously worked at a medical call centre assisting patients with chronic pain and is now working at a coffee shop.

**Hanako Teranishi** (they/them) is an MA student at Simon Fraser University. They are a writer, poet, and writing tutor. They volunteer with multiple Japanese Canadian community organizations. Their first jobs were in the food and service industry. They worked at a Japanese restaurant in Winnipeg for four years as a server.

**Zahra Tootonsab** is a poet-activist and PhD candidate at McMaster University. Her doctoral project uses poetry to explore the relationship between water, sheltering, and decolonial flourishing from so-called Canada to Iran. Her work (in/with/about community) embodies how decolonial sheltering/living can address the challenges of the global climate crisis.

**Jennifer Wickham** is a Cas Yikh (Grizzly House) member of the Gidimt'en (Bear/Wolf) clan of the Wet'suwet'en nation. She has been writing poetry since childhood and has published one collection titled *I'm a Real Skin* (2013). She is an artist, trained high school educator, director/producer of *YINTAH* (2024), and Gidimt'en Checkpoint Media Coordinator.

**Evan Woelk Balzer** is a project coordinator at the Nature Conservancy of Canada, where he facilitates prairie grassland stewardship across Alberta, Saskatchewan, and Manitoba. He works collaboratively with cattle producers, Indigenous communities, and ENGOs, among others, to pursue a thriving future for Canada's prairie grasslands.

## THE LAND AND LABOUR POETRY COLLECTIVE

**Moni Brar** comes from a long lineage of subsistence farmers and has worked in 14 countries. She has worked as a fruit picker, tree sorter, customs officer, academic, swamper, and international consultant. She is a winner of *The Fiddlehead*'s Poetry Prize and the Lieutenant Governor of Alberta Emerging Artist Award.

**Jenna Butler** (she/her) is the author of six books of poetry and creative nonfiction, including *Revery: A Year of Bees,* finalist for the 2021 Governor General's Award for Nonfiction. Butler works as a writing teacher, editor, and off-grid organic farmer in northern Treaty 6.

**Samantha F. Jones** is a poet, editor, and earth scientist based in Moh'kins'tsis (Calgary, Alberta). She is Black Canadian and white settler with roots in Nova Scotia, Québec, and Ontario. Her poetry collection, *Attic Rain* (2024), is available from NeWest Press. Sam is currently a University of Calgary PhD Candidate researching Arctic carbon cycling.

**Jamie Paris** (he/him) is an English literature Instructor in Winnipeg, at the University of Manitoba, where he teaches students about poetry, the works of William Shakespeare, and critical race theory. He is a mixed-race (Black, Scottish, and Métis), neurodiverse writer whose creative work has previously appeared in *Prairie Fire*.

**Kelly Shepherd** used to work in construction; "Mothballing Mould Bay" is about environmental cleanup in the North. His third poetry collection, *Dog and Moon*, was published by Oskana in 2025. *Insomnia Bird* (Thistledown, 2018), his second, won the 2019 Robert Kroetsch City of Edmonton Book Prize. Originally from Smithers, BC, Kelly lives on Treaty 6 territory, in Edmonton.

**Melanie Dennis Unrau** is a white-settler poet, editor, scholar, parent, and climate organizer from Treaty One territory and Métis homeland in Winnipeg. She is the author of *Goose* (Assembly, 2025), *The Rough Poets: Reading Oil-Worker Poetry* (MQUP, 2024), and *Happiness Threads: The Unborn Poems* (The Muses' Company, 2013).

## CREDITS

Some poems in this book have been previously published or are forthcoming in chapbooks, books, or literary journals. All are used with permission.

**p. 3** "Tools — A Litany" by Jane Byers is forthcoming in *Coming Home from the Candy Factory* (Caitlin Press, 2025).

**p. 4** "What If I Told You" by Jennifer Wickham was first published as part of a forum in *Canadian Literature*, 251 (2022): 163–68.

**p. 6** "remind me one more time" by Moni Brar was first published in *Contemporary Verse 2* 46, 1 (2023): 36–37; and in the chapbook *Migrant Wish* (Sundress Publications, 2024).

**p. 44** "Peasant Urbanite" by Sanita Fejzić is forthcoming in *Refugee Mouth* (Frontenac House, 2025).

**p. 50** "Mothballing Mould Bay, NWT" by Kelly Shepherd was first published in *Shift* (Thistledown, 2016).

**p. 57** "Carbon Offsets" by Rina Garcia Chua was first published in *GUEST* 17 (2021).

**p. 79** "Professional Experience" by Jessica Bebenek was first published in *The Humber Literary Review* 2, 2 (2024): 15.

**p. 84** An earlier version of "The Aftermath" by Peace Akintade-Oluwagbeye was first published in the self-published chapbook *Equanimity In Sonder* (2024).

**p. 86** "Arctic Adoration" by Ashley Qilavaq-Savard was first published in *Where the Sea Kuniks the Land* (Inhabit Media, 2023).

**p. 94** "A Distorted Portrait" by Paul Akpomuje is forthcoming in *Black Passport* (Griots Lounge Canada, 2025).

**p. 96** "inventory" by Christina Shah was first published in *Rig Veda* (Anstruther, 2023).

**p. 99** "Those Days before the Mine" by Jon Broderick was first published in *The FisherPoets Gathering Songbook* (FisherPoets Gathering, 2020).

p. **108** "There Has Been Something" by Ed Edmo was first published in *Yon's Ma Life: Poetry and Art from People Who Work the Sea* (FisherPoets Gathering, 2022).

## ENDNOTES

1. Audre Lorde, "Poetry Is Not a Luxury," in *Sister Outsider: Essays and Speeches by Audre Lorde* (Freedom, CA: The Crossing Press, 1984), 39.
2. Kobayashi Takiji, qtd. by Komori Yōichi, "Introduction," in *The Crab Cannery Ship and Other Novels of Struggle*, by Kobayashi Takiji, trans. Željko Cipriš (Honolulu: University of Hawaiʻi Press, 2013), 2.
3. Leanne Betasamosake Simpson, *The Gift Is in the Making: Anishinaabeg Stories* (Winnipeg: HighWater Press, 2013).
4. Tom Wayman (ed.), *A Government Job at Last: An Anthology of Working Poems, Mainly Canadian* (Vancouver: MacLeod Books, 1976); Tom Wayman (ed.), *Going for Coffee: Poetry on the Job* (Madeira Park: Harbour Publishing, 1981); Tom Wayman (ed.), *Paperwork: An Anthology* (Madeira Park: Harbour Publishing, 1991).
5. Tom Wayman, *If You're Not Free at Work, Where Are You Free? Literature and Social Change, Selected Essays and Interviews 1994–2014* (Toronto: Guernica Editions, 2018).
6. Alicia Elliott, "CanLit Is a Raging Dumpster Fire," in *Refuse: CanLit in Ruins*, eds. Hannah McGregor, Julie Rak, and Erin Wunker (Toronto: Book*hug, 2018), 93–98.
7. Jen Currin, Jordan Hall, Ray Hsu, Christine Leclerc, Nikki Reimer, Melissa Sawatsky, and Daniel Zomparelli (eds.), *The Enpipe Line: 70,000+ Kilometres of Poetry Written in Resistance to the Enbridge Northern Gateway Pipelines Proposal* (Smithers: Creekstone Press, 2012).
8. Kathryn Mockler, Madhur Anand, Stephen Collis, Jennifer Dorner, Catherine Graham, Elena Johnson, Canisia Lubrin, Kim Mannix, June Pak, Sina Queyras, Shazia Hafiz Ramji, Rasiqra Revulva, Yusuf Saadi, Sanchari Sur, and Jacqueline Valencia (eds.), *Watch Your Head: Writers & Artists Respond to the Climate Crisis* (Toronto: Coach House Books, 2020).
9. Amber Dawn and Justin Ducharme (eds.), *Hustling Verse: An Anthology of Sex Workers' Poetry* (Vancouver: Arsenal Pulp Press, 2019).
10. Shane Neilson, Sarah Fraser, and Arundhati Dhara (eds.), *The COVID Journals: Health Care Workers Write the Pandemic* (Edmonton: University of Alberta Press, 2023).
11. Mark Nowak, *Social Poetics* (Minneapolis: Coffee House Press, 2020).
12. Hari Alluri, "Blessing Wednesday," in *We Were Not Alone*, eds. Hari Alluri and Seema Reza (Community Building Art Works, 2021), 26–27. The quotation in the epigraph is used with permission.